Sex Positions

The Best Quick Guide for Exploding Couple's Sex Life with The Best Sex Positions

Couples Sex Guide with DEMONSTRATED SEX POSITIONS

Disclaimer

While all attempts have been made to provide effective, verifiable information in this Book, neither the Author nor Publisher assumes any responsibility for errors, inaccuracies, or omissions. Any slights of people or organizations are unintentional.

This Book is not a source of medical information, and it should not be regarded as such. This publication is designed to provide accurate and authoritative information in regard to the subject matter covered. It is sold with the understanding that the publisher is not engaged in rendering a medical service. As with any medical advice, the reader is strongly encouraged to seek professional medical advice before taking action.

WARNING

This book is for sale to **ADULTS ONLY**. It contains substantial sexually explicit scenes and graphic language which may be considered offensive by some readers. Please store your book where it cannot be accessed by minors.

To the Reader

Scientific research does prove that the chemistry of brand new love does have a shelf life. Psychology Today reports that researches suggest the first thrill of sex-related enthusiasm can last 4 to 15 months. It's not long lasting, what a pity. Yet there's no reason to worry in the towel right now. With the appropriate guide and also some imagination, you can develop a terrific article crush magnetism that will get you in the state of mind for sex and maintain you there.

The largest blunder you can make is lacking ideas to maintain your connection & sex life hot. This sex guide covers more than 100 sex positions which can assist you develop a more intimate connection as you spice things up. It likewise includes expert demos of every single placement a lot of the m simple as well as really imaginative to do. This guide is for couples who wish to delight in, treasure as well as check out each other understanding that there still is a sexual mystery left in each other hence only intimacy can reveal the treasure. Have your guy or girl constantly think of you ... even if you've been wed for the last 10 years.

For guys available, you do not need an additional lady to have something new; the exact same one has a great deal to provide when sex is an experience through this Guide changing that preliminary spark.

Ladies you do not require parts for your man to see something new. Attempt these out also as well as stun him as well as bear in mind sex is best when its two way so ENJOY!

Introduction

Sparks fade. Enthusiasm dampens. Life 'happens'. That's the course most relationships take. What if you could picked a various path? Among extreme interest, addicting sexual stress & having a person who regularly thinking of you ... even if you've been wed for the last 10 years? This checks out the eleven groups of sex-related positions and each group having numerous neighborhoods making the overall to be more than a hundred. Out of the total every day you can attempt each, no requirement to hurry with, take it simple as well as slow - enlivening your relationship with the expectation of something various with each day. The groups are as adheres to: Girl on Top

Sitting Sex Positions, Standing Sex Positions, Exotic Sex Positions, Lying on Your Side Sex Positions, Lying on Your Back Sex Positions, Lying on Your Stomach Sex Positions, Doggy Style Sex Positions, Kneeling Sex Positions, Sitting down On Your Man's Lap Sex Positions, 69 Sex Positions.

Chapter 1. Girl on Top sex positions

If your guy is constantly ahead throughout sex or in the 'dominant' position, after that straddling him is a terrific means to change things up and take on a more dominant role on your own

Getting on leading and also taking control can be actually enjoyable! The placements on this design are: Amazon Position, Asian Cowgirl Position, Bucking Bronco Position, Corner Cowgirl Position, Cowgirl Position, Crab Position, Fast Fuck Position, Jugghead Position, Lunge Position, Man Missionary Position, Reverse Cowgirl Position, Rodeo Position, Sliding Lady Position, Sybian Position, as well as Thigh Tide Position

1a. Amazon Sex Position

The Amazon sex placement is a woman on the top setting that a great deal of people have actually never really heard of. It's really enjoyable and also certainly worth trying, particularly if you like to take on a somewhat dominant role in the bed room.

To do the Amazon, your male needs to rest on his back and bring his legs upwards as well as bend his knees. You after that need to squat down on your male, while he pulls his legs near to his upper body so that they are out of your method. You then simply need to squat up and down to allow him to permeate you. You will discover that your male will naturally press you back upwards with his upper legs.

You may discover entering into this position to be a little difficult initially, yet its well worth it if you like getting on top.

When executing this position, you require to be mindful not to unintentionally injure your man's penis as it will be flexing in reverse rather a whole lot.

Woman roles

Your very first top priority is obtaining right into position without harming your man and also making certain that you are comfortable when you are executing the Amazon with your male. You may discover that leaning on your man's thighs helps to take the stress off your legs a little.

I advise that you initially get into position above your male, prior to taking his penis into your vagina. When remain in setting, slowly draw it backwards and then slide it inside. With the very first couple of strokes, ensure that you are careful and also very mild so as not to harm your male. See to it to ask him how it really feels as well as go from there.

Male Roles

When your man remains in the Amazon placement, he will not be doing a lot. He needs to have a small amount of flexibility so that he can really hold his legs right into his breast as well as out of your method. He can utilize his thighs to extremely gently assist to nudge you up and down on his penis.

It can really feel like he is attempting to push you off if your male is not that adaptable him.

Variants

There are a variety of variations of the Amazon that you can perform if you discover that the routine Amazon is awkward or also hard to do.

Stooping-- Instead of crouching over your guy, try kneeling to take the pressure off your legs, the only issue with stooping is that you may find yourself regularly slipping down the back of your male's upper legs which will certainly better bend his penis in reverse.

Opposite-- Performing the Amazon in reverse (by having your back to your guy), you may discover it to be much, a lot easier. You will be sort of remaining on your man's thighs while jumping backwards and forwards on him.

Tips

The more you lean over your male (in the regular Amazon setting), the less pressure you will be putting on his suspensory tendons in his penis (the much less stressed his penis will be).

The Reverse Amazon is much easier to carry out with your guy, without seeming like his thighs are constantly pressing you off.

Comments

The Amazon position is a somewhat extra unique setting to carry out with your partner. If you like tackling a dominant role, where you have a lot of the control, then you have reached try it

1b. Asian Cowgirl Sex Position

The oriental cowgirl sex setting is very comparable to routine the routine cowgirl position. You get on top, while your man is resting on his back. However there are still some significant distinctions that you require to consider when performing it.

In the normal cowgirl setting, you will have your knees either side of your man, resting on the bed. When you are doing the eastern cowgirl with your man, you will be squatting, which suggests that the majority of your weight will be sustained by your feet while you are crouching. You can utilize your hands to take a few of your weight by placing them on either your guy's upper body or on either side of him on the bed. If you are not extremely solid or adaptable, you will certainly find the eastern cowgirl position to be promptly tiring.

You can lean forward or backward or remain upright like in this demonstration of the Asian Cowgirl.

Lady Roles

When you remain in the asian cowgirl placement, you will certainly be crouching over your man. I find that it's best to begin with the regular cowgirl position and then transition into eastern cowgirl. To relocate into asian cowgirl from routine cowgirl, very first lean forwards as well as place your hands on the bed to steady yourself. Next rock back onto your toes as well as increase your body just off your guy to enter into the squatting placement.

Currently put your hands on your man upper body as well as together utilizing both your legs and also arms, slowly rise up and also down. Switch to utilizing your legs and vice-versa if you discover that your arms are getting tired from doing many of the work. Certainly you can change the angle of entry by either leaning forwards or in reverse. Nonetheless if you lean backwards too much, you may locate that it's more difficult to balance and also your legs obtain tired even much faster.

Male Roles

Your guy will certainly have a lot less job to do when you are in the asian cowgirl position. If he wants, he can simply lie there and also literally not do anything whatsoever. But that's not what great sex is all about. If he assists you to bounce up and also down, what's ideal is. Simply put he can put his hands under your legs/bum and also assistance to lift you backwards and forwards, so that you are refraining every one of the job. He can put a hand on either side of your waistline to balance you.

Tips

If you discover that you tire swiftly in the Asian cowgirl setting, after that a wonderful means to last much longer is to try and also stay consistent in one placement, while your guy does all the thrusting.

The most effective means to last longer is to utilize the Top Tip above: Hold still, while your male does all the thrusting.

You require a good level of adaptability and stamina to do the oriental cowgirl.

You can make use of a firm pillow or 2 under your bum to ensure that your legs are no longer taking all the weight. Make sure to obtain your man to maintain his legs with each other if you do this, or else the pillows will not be of much usage.

Comments

If your man has the ability to drive really swiftly, women can get a lot of enjoyment from it when they stay consistent in one position.

1c. Throwing Bronco Sex Position

If you like being on leading as well as having many of the control throughout sex, the Bucking Bronco sex setting is great. The Bucking Bronco is rather comparable to the Octopus setting yet is a lot easier and also much less tiring to do.

To set on your own up in the Bucking Bronco placement, your man requires to rest on his back. You then need to jump on top of him, facing him. When he is inside you, lean backwards and also place your arms behind you to keep yourself balanced. Put your feet so that they are either side of your guy's head. The broader you spread your feet, the less complicated it will be to stabilize on your own.

Transitioning to the Bucking Bronco setting from Asian Cowgirl is truly very easy.

Now you will certainly be able to bounce backwards and forwards on your guy, much like a. ... Bucking Bronco. You'll locate that it's quite simple to switch to the Bucking Bronco from the Reverse Cowgirl position.

Girl roles

When you are doing the Bucking Bronco with your man, you will certainly be doing most of the job, lifting yourself backwards and forwards on your male. This will rapidly get tiring if your guy is not aiding you out. To pause, attempt sitting right down on your guy as well as rocking yourself backwards and forwards.

The Bucking Bronco is also a wonderful setting for rectal sex. If you are having anal sex while doing it, after that you can use one hand to massage your clitoris and also vaginal canal and even finger yourself, while utilizing your other hand to stabilize yourself

Male roles

He doesn't have to do anything if your male is specifically lazy. Yet if he has an interest in both of you enjoying, then he needs to be energetic as well. Keeping his legs directly and together won't allow him to propelled right into you with much pressure. Instead, he needs to lift his knees and bend them a little bit, then plant them on the bed. This will certainly enable him to get take advantage of as well as thrust harder.

He can additionally simply gyrate his hips while staying deep inside you.

Tips

If you locate that your shoulders/arms quickly burn out, after that try leaning back further and also rest on your joints rather. Simply take care as you will certainly be placing additional stress on your male's penis.

Alternatively, attempt leaning more forward.

A third alternative is for your guy to raise his knees up far enough to make sure that you can comfortably exist back on them so you currently longer need to utilize your arms to support on your own.

There is an excellent little space for you to move around in the Bucking Bronco positions, so make certain to experiment a little bit up until you locate an angle that you really enjoy.

Comments

It's more enjoyable and also a little less tough or exhausting for you to just grind in this placement as opposed to jumping up and down.

1d. Corner Cowgirl Sex Position

The Corner Cowgirl sex placement is clearly a variant of the routine Cowgirl sex positions, where you get on top of your male at the corner of the bed, while he's pushing his back. This is an excellent placement to try if you are obtaining bored of routine Cowgirl.

To perform it, your male requires to lie on his back on the bed. His crotch must be placed by the edge of the bed, to ensure that among his legs dangles over 1 side of the bed, while the various other dangles over the end of the bed.

Preferably your male must plant his feet on the floor to give himself some security. You then require to straddle him as you usually would when executing the cowgirl positions to ensure that you are on your knees, "bouncing" up and down on him.

Lady roles

When you are on top of your guy, on your knees, part of your lower legs will certainly be hanging over the edge of the bed.

Your very first objective is a security one: you require to be careful not to accidentally slide backwards as well as fall off him.

To see to it you do not, try leaning ahead a bit in addition to your guy. As opposed to just "jumping" up and down on your guy, you might locate it a little bit a lot more enjoyable to sit right down on him as well as move your hips forwards as well as backwards to ensure that you are grinding on him with really little thrusting.

Guy roles

When your male is pushing his back, he has the option of relaxing and also allowing you do the majority of the job, however actually he needs to be doing his reasonable share if he is serious about fantastic sex.

If the bed goes to the best elevation and his feet are planted on the floor, it implies that he can propelled up right into you fairly intensely, while you keep on your own a little elevated on your knees. He can likewise put his hands on your hips as well as press you forwards and backwards to grind on him.

Tips

The first thing is to see to it that you do not slip in reverse and inadvertently diminish. An excellent wat to avoid on your own from falling off is simply to obtain your man to relocate additionally back in the direction of the center of the bed so that just his reduced legs are hanging over the side.

As with the majority of sex positions, ensure to do a little trial and error by leaning forwards and also in reverse to locate an angle that you actually delight in.

If your bed has both a headboard and footboard, you will not be able to perform it.

Remarks

It's easy to transition to from Cowgirl or Asian Cowgirl for more passionate sex.

1e. Cowgirl Sex Position

Cowgirl is probably the single most well-known 'girl on top' sex positions there is. And also, it's truly simple to execute. Simply have a look at the picture below. If you have actually never ever been 'on the top' prior to, the cowgirl placement is a fantastic area to start. If your guy is normally the one on top and also calling the shots, the fantastic point regarding cowgirl is that you are currently the one in control which can be actually enjoyable.

Like being on top and also remaining in control? You'll like Cowgirl!

As I claimed, this is an extremely very easy positions to have sex in. Your guy simply requires to just lay on his back while you straddle him with your legs either side of his waist to make sure that your knees get on the bed. You can place you hands on his chest, shoulders or the bed to constant on your own or alternatively you can simply put them on your upper legs.

Male Roles

The man doesn't actually need to do anything in the cowgirl position. However to be honest that's not what sex is about! While the man is resting on his back, he can merely propelled backwards and forwards. Or he can gradually gyrate his hips in a swirling motion to promote the wall of your vaginal area. Or he can attempt doing both at the same time.

If your are obtaining exhausted, your man can likewise put his hands under your bottom and assistance to press you up and down.

Lady Roles

When you are in the cowgirl positions you are actually the one in control. You can jump backwards and forwards on your guy's penis or instead, you can relocate your body forwards as well as backwards to boost your clitoris et cetera of the beyond your vagina. Think of it as grinding against his pubic bone. Or you can try doing both at the same time.

You'll also locate that by leaning forwards or backwards you can alter the angle of access. If you discover that you are leaning back a great deal, then make sure to utilize your hands to assist steady on your own.

Your guy can aid you to grind on him utilizing his hands like in the picture over.

Tips

It's completely natural to be a little bit anxious the very first few times you try it. To assist take the stress off, try doing it with the lights off. Some women find that leaning in on top of the ir man towards his face assists to take the pressure off while also being quite intimate at the very same time.

You don't need to be especially flexible to do the cowgirl. But if you are leaning in reverse a whole lot, then it's a great idea to be at the very least a little versatile.

Keep adjusting your placement by moving your hips backwards and forwards in addition to leaning your entire body either backwards or forwards up until you discover a placement that you truly appreciate.

Although your guy might not appreciate it that much, a lot of women I have actually spoken to have claimed that they actually appreciate 'grinding' to stimulate their clitoris in this position while their guy is still inside them. Numerous have claimed that they a lot like this to just jumping backwards and forwards on his cock.

Sometimes your man will not get much out of this position. So be aware of this and make sure to change positions from the cowgirl to something that your man delights in if he does not appear to like it that a lot. Bear in mind sex has to do with 2 people (or even more!) having a fun time. It's never ever cool to be egocentric throughout sex.

Comments

If you like being submissive throughout sex, cowgirl isn't an especially passive placement.

1f. Crab Sex Position

The crab sex placement is a placement that I just suggest you attempt if your male has a bargain of penile adaptability. This is due to the fact that you will certainly be bending his penis rather far back when you remain on him.

In many aspects, the Crab Sex Position resembles the Cowgirl placement, with you on your knees on top, encountering your male while he is lying on his back. Rather of you being in a relatively upright placement on top of your man, you will certainly be leaning right back. Make certain that you stretch your give out behind you to support yourself in this position. Your male ought to keep his legs with each other.

You'll see that the Crab placement is very similar to the Bucking Bronco, other than that in the Crab, your body is a lot more 'stretched out'.

When you are in this placement, his penis will certainly be stimulating the upper wall surface of your vagina a whole lot more than if you were simply doing the routine Cowgirl and even Asian Cowgirl.

Woman roles

In the Crab positions, you will be leaning ideal backwards, supporting yourself on the bed with your hands behind your back. When you are first getting involved in this position, it's important to gradually reduce yourself in reverse so as not to mistakenly harm your guy by overstraining his penis.

Once you are in positions, you simply need to gradually bring your body backwards and forwards. Use both your legs and arms to achieve this. You can likewise grind on him by thrusting your hips forwards and also in reverse. Once again make sure to start off doing this really gradually to prevent yourself from mistakenly hurting your male.

Man roles

One of the most essential job for your man in the Crab positions is to allow you recognize just how he feels. He requires to tell you promptly if you are placing way too much stress on his penis. When he is comfortable, after that he can begin to enjoy himself a whole lot a lot more. He can begin returning right into you. Or if you are grinding on him, after that he can grab your hips and also aid relocate you back as well as ahead. To assist sustain you, your man can increase his legs somewhat as well as flex his knees to make sure that you can rest part of your weight on his thighs as opposed to having your hands carry all your weight.

Tips

As the Crab position is quite very easy to execute by transitioning to it from routine Cowgirl

- Better Safe Than Sorry: It's truly essential that you relieve yourself into this positions with your man. Sex is not expected to painful for either of you, so in the beginning make certain that your male is not in any kind of discomfort.

- Your male can aid regulate exactly how much you lean back by using his legs.

- Sometimes you will certainly obtain a lot more satisfaction out of this position by simply grinding as well as revolving your hips when in addition to your man instead of taking him in and out.

Comments

The Crab position is absolutely a little a lot more unique than the majority of sex positions, however it can be unbelievably pleasurable for those that like having their G-Spot promoted by their male. The trick is discovering the right deepness of penetration and angle for maximum enjoyment and enjoyment.

1g. Quick Fuck Sex Position

When you desire a quickie with your male, the Fast Fuck sex position is great for. As the name suggests, the Fast Fuck includes your male quickly thrusting in and out. In a lot of means, the Fast Fuck is rather comparable to the Cowgirl or perhaps the Asian Cowgirl positions.

To set it up, your male just requires to lie down on his back and also flex his knees slightly with his feet grown on the ground. You after that need to straddle him. You have an option of being on your knees or on your feet. It's up to you. You will be leaning ahead, resting on your arm joints or hands. You require to place on your own so that you are a little raised over your man.

Moving from Asian Cowgirl into the Fast Fuck position is all-natural & truly simple.

You will not be hing on your man's crotch in any way. He will then start trusting backwards and forwards actually quickly. The penetration won't be very deep, yet it feels terrific for your man.

Woman roles

You will typically remain in the Fast Fuck positions for only regarding 1-3 mins prior to your man gets either too exhausted or he climaxes and ejaculates. The whole time that you remain in this position, you just require to maintain your body in a fixed placement, increased over your male and never ever hing on him. For some, they find it less complicated to be on their knees, while others will certainly discover that bending on their feet like in the Asian Cowgirl positions.

Man roles

Your male will certainly get on his back, with his legs slightly bent and his feet planted on the flooring. This will certainly give him the take advantage of needed to rapidly penetrate you. In this position, all your male requires to do is embeded and out. Because you won't be resting on him whatsoever, there will certainly be really little resistance for your guy. Which's it. There is nothing else that he requires to do in this position.

If he locates that he is getting tired, then he can alter the angle he is flexing his knees at or even correct them out.

Tips

The Fast Fuck is perfect for quickies. The Fast Fuck really feels terrific for your guy, whatever angle he enters you at, yet you require to do a little trial and error with just how your position yourself (on your knees/feet/how far onward you lean over) to find a spot that you actually take pleasure in.

The Fast Fuck normally does not really feel great for rectal sex unless you make use of big amounts of lube.

One downside to the Fast Fuck is that it's not specifically intimate. You won't be making a great deal of physical contact with your guy throughout it.

Remarks

it's not a wonderful position to use for intimate, sensuous sex with your girl.

1h. Jugghead Sex Position

The Jugghead placement is most likely the craziest looking love making even though doing it is not that tough.

Positions yourselves in the Jugghead positions is rather easy. You are mosting likely to need to use either a couch or a bed to perform it. Your guy needs to establish himself up. He needs to rest next to the bed/couch with his back on the flooring.

The Jugghead position is great if you like getting on leading and also in control!

He then requires to put his boosts on the sofa/bed. You now need to place yourself above him on all fours with one arm and also one leg on either side of him. Your guy then requires to lift his crotch and also reduced withdraw the flooring and afterwards begin penetrating you, while you thrust back onto him.

Woman roles

When you are in the Jugghead position, you have a selection:
1) You can be fairly active and also push back on to your male with each drive
or
2) You can remain fairly still and also just allow him fuck you, yet you'll find that your guy only has a restricted range of activity when he's in the Jugghead position. Certainly you can do various other things too, like kissing your guy or scrubing your clit to assist you orgasm or even thumbing on your own if you are having anal sex with your guy.

Guy roles

The first time your guy remains in the Jugghead placement, he will discover it fairly uncomfortable and a little unusual also. So it may take him a while to get used to it. Once he fits, then he can begin propelling right into. Besides thrusting right into you, your man is not in a placement to do much else. But that's about it if he likes then he can use his hands to massage your breasts.

Tips

The bed/sofa that you try the Jugghead on needs to have room below it to put your legs, otherwise you will have to squat right to do it with your guy.

The Jugghead does not permit much variation. You and also your man will both discover that you cannot transform your positioning that easily to alter the angle of entry.

Anal sex is feasible in the Jugghead placement.

You can utilize the Jugghead for carrying out the 69 with your man. You just need reverse so that your vaginal area is above his mouth and your mouth is above his penis.

Ideas

Its excellent fun to use it from time to time to spice points up in the room as well as stop things from obtaining boring. However don't simply listen to me before determining to try the Jugghead positions. You require to experiment yourself as well as try it out prior to deciding whether or not it's for you.

1i. Lunge Sex Position

The Lunge sex positions gets it's name from the reality that you will be lunging in addition to your male while executing it. This indicates that you require to have a little of versatility and also stamina if you intend to perform the Lunge for a long duration with your guy.

As you can see in the picture, the Lunge positions calls for a reasonable degree of adaptability and also toughness. Or else you will certainly get tired, quick.

To enter the Lunge position, your guy needs to lie down on the bed on his back and he needs to open his legs. You are after that going to get right into a lunging position on top of him. To do this, start off by standing up right on the bed, facing your guy with your feet together just below his crotch with your feet inside his legs.

Currently take your left foot and place it to the side of your man's ideal arm on the bed. Next place your right leg in reverse behind yourself so that you remain in the lunging positions and also lower on your own onto your guy. With the help of your male, slowly lower and increase yourself on your male while he is inside you.

Girl roles

When you are doing the Lunge with your man, you can relocate yourself up and down making use of both your legs, but you'll obtain extremely exhausted doing this. Rather, you should put your hands on your guy and utilize them to move on your own up and down. You must use your hips to thrust in and out of him.

Switch your legs around so that your other foot is now to the side of his other arm if your find your legs getting sore and tired.

Male roles

Your guy may believe that he can simply lie back as well as take pleasure in the flight, but it's a rather strenuous position as well as he should be assisting. He must additionally be returning into you. He can utilize his arms to grab you by the waist and also aid to lift you backwards and forwards on him if you like.

You can even take a rest as well as sit right down on top of your man as well as allow him take duty for thrusting as well as grinding.

Tips

If you just utilize your arms and your man assists, you do not need to use your legs that a lot in any way to raise on your own up and down, allowing you to make love in the Lunge for a lot longer prior to your legs obtain tired.

Your male can do the Lunge with his legs together instead of having them open.

Comments

The Lunge position is commonly viewed as an uniqueness by some people and also is right away dismissed by them. I recommend that you try it on your own before determining whether it's something for you and also your man.

1j. Male Missionary Sex Position

The Man Missionary position is the precise opposite to the Missionary positions. Instead of your male getting on top, you are.

To set up the Man Missionary positions, your guy needs to relax on his back with his legs with each other. They can be straight or he can flex them a little bit at the knee. You after that require to straddle him such as in the Cowgirl position with your knees on the bed, facing him. You then require to lean onward over your male and also rest on your elbows or hands or just relax your whole body on his belly and breast. You can then shake to and fro in addition to your man. It's just like the Missionary position, but upside down.

Below you can see our pair executing the Man Missionary with our male design bending his knees.

Woman roles

You can be as active as you like in the Man Missionary sex positions. You can allow your guy thrust from below while you just lie on top of him. Or you can gently grind on him. Or you can be much more energetic as well as utilize your hips to jump up and down on him.

As you are leaning over your man you will have the ability to kiss him as well as get truly near to him for intimacy. If you wish to seasoning points up a little and also take even more control, then you can try getting his arms as well as pinning them over his head. Moving from the regular Cowgirl placement to the Man Missionary is simple. All you need to do is just lean ahead over your man.

To get even more clitoral excitement, attempt pulling your crotch towards your top body like you are doing a crunch.

Male roles
Your man also has a selection of just how active he wishes to remain in the Man Missionary position. He can just exist there and also allow you grind as well as bounce backwards and forwards on him. Or he can bend his knees somewhat to provide him enough utilize to thrust into you. If he likes, he can put his arms around you to draw you right into him.

Tips
If you don't like being on top, - You may feel a little uncomfortable in the Man Missionary position

- You can obtain some really terrific clitoral stimulation if you angle your body right as well as grind up against your man as he propelling right into you.

- The Man Missionary position can be truly intimate if you just lie right down on your male and gently rock and also grind on each other.

Comments
The Man Missionary is really similar to both routine Missionary positions as well as the Cowgirl positions, but even with these similarities, it's not in fact that preferred. The next time you are doing Cowgirl with your man, try leaning onward and entering into the Man Missionary to see if you appreciate it.

1k. Reverse Cowgirl Sex Position

The Reverse Cowgirl sex position is among the a lot more well known sex positions around. It's excellent for those that such as getting on top of the ir male, however do not intend to invest all your time checking into his eyes.

Entering the Reverse Cowgirl position is simple and luckily doesn't call for a huge amount of adaptability. Your guy initially needs to start by lying down on his back. You after that need to get onto your knees, with one on either side of him, over his lap to ensure that he is encountering your back. Then just lower on your own down on him.

Reverse Cowgirl is a terrific position to try the very first time you get on top of your male throughout sex.

You can after that start to slowly grind on him or you can begin jumping up and down. In numerous methods, the Reverse Cowgirl position is really similar to both the Acrobat and also Bucking Bronco sex positions.

Girl roles

Among the most effective features of the Reverse Cowgirl placement that makes it easier for those who are a little shy or worried getting on top is that you do not have to face your male while executing it, which takes a lot of the 'efficiency stress' or anxiety out of the equation that some girls feel when on top of the ir guy. As soon as you get comfy getting on top of your male, there is a couple of things you must experiment with. Try out leaning either forwards or in reverse (utilizing your hand to sustain on your own) to change the angle if entrance. You also have the choice of either grinding on your guy or bouncing backwards and forwards on him or a combination of both.

Male roles

Your man can pick to take either an active or extra passive role throughout Reverse Cowgirl. He can exist there while you do all the work or he can become more entailed. He can grind back up against you as you are grinding on him if he wants to become more involved. Or he can thrust backwards and forwards. If you want lean back towards your guy after that you can utilize his arms to support you.

Tips

Try doing it before a mirror. The great thing about executing the Reverse Cowgirl positions before a mirror is that you can see every little thing you're doing, while your man is obscured.

Try doing Reverse Asian Cowgirl. This is just a combination of the Reverse Cowgirl as well as Asian Cowgirl placements.

Reverse Cowgirl is excellent for anal sex along with normal genital sex.

Comments

It's an easy and nice variation of the routine Cowgirl placement. If you are one of those that find themselves really feeling uncomfortable or a little anxious getting on top of the ir guy, then you must try Reverse Cowgirl, as you do not have to fret about making eye contact with him.

1l. Rodeo Sex Position

When performing it with your man, the Rodeo position gets it's name from the fact that you often look like you are performing in a rodeo. The Rodeo sex position is more like the Cowgirl position, but with you facing in the opposite direction.

You'll find that the Rodeo is extra like a video game than a sex position!

To set up the Rodeo, your man first needs to lie down on the bed on his back. You then require to get on top of him, straddling him to ensure that you are dealing with towards his feet with your back to him.

You will get on your knees, upright while in addition to your guy. After that you can begin to go up as well as down on his penis or you can grind on it. Your male will be propelling up into you. If he thrusts actually hard, after that it can truly start to feel like a rodeo as if your man is attempting to 'throw' you off him.

Woman role

As you will be on top of your guy, you will certainly be rather energetic when in the Rodeo placement. This implies that you can merely move forward and also back over your guy, while he stays inside you. This will cause his penis to promote many different areas inside your vagina.

You can additionally 'jump' backwards and forwards on your guy utilizing your legs. If you are obtaining tired from jumping up and down on your guy, after that attempt leaning forward as well as relaxing your hands on his legs while using your hips to jump up and down on his penis. Do not place your hands on his knees as this can cause injury!

Male roles

Your man can simply lay there like a dead fish. That doesn't feel so good for you. As he doesn't have as much mobility as you do, due you getting on top of him, he can actually only propelled backwards and forwards into you when he's in the Rodeo positions. He can alternate how fast and hard he thrusts. He can thrust really rapidly into you just like during the Fast fuck if you raise yourself slightly above him. He can also get you by the waist and also relocate you forward and also backwards, aiding you to grind on him.

Tips

Changing your angle while he is propelling right into you is important to find a great area. Attempt leaning right back on your male up until you are in the Acrobat placement. Try leaning really far forwards with your hands in front of you.

You remain in the perfect position to give on your own with a little manual excitement while in the Rodeo placement.

Remarks

It's super-simple to do as well as it makes for a superb adjustment from something like regular Cowgirl.

1m. Gliding Lady Sex Position

The Sliding Lady is sort of like a reverse form of the Coital Alignment Technique (CAT). Instead of your male being on top, you are.

While the Sliding Lady looks a little unpleasant, it can be incredibly enjoyable!
To establish the Sliding Lady, your man requires to lie down on his back as if he was performing the Asian Cowgirl or the Side Saddle positions. You then need to straddle him as you would when doing the Cowgirl placement. So you will certainly get on your knees on top of your man, facing him. Next you require to lean over him and also rest your weight on your hands. This next part is the most vital:
You then require to position on your own to make sure that your clitoris is in contact with your man's pubic bone. You can see our women model do this by arching her back like a feline.

Girl roles
When in the Sliding Lady placement, you are not going to concentrate on going up and also down on your male. Rather you are going to be concentrating on relocating forwards and also backwards over your male, while he stays within you. This is to make sure that you obtain a lot of clitoral stimulation.
You'll find that it's simpler to do this by arching your back or by performing a type of 'ab crisis' activity. Different points help various individuals, so my suggestions is to experiment with relocating your body in a great deal of various variants to see what offers you the most complete satisfaction and satisfaction.

Male roles
Your male does not have a whole lot he is going perform in the Sliding Lady position. He simply needs to exist there. He can experiment with gently grinding up against you to see if it's more satisfying. He can additionally put his hands on your hips to aid rock you backwards and forwards while you are grinding on him.

Tips
- You might locate that you have to experiment with an excellent few somewhat various variations when carrying out the Sliding Lady up until you locate something that feels perfect.
- You can attempt making use of a vibe when performing the Sliding Lady with your man.
- Better yet, your guy can attempt using a vibrating cock ring when performing the Sliding Lady.

Remarks

When preforming sliding woman it's actually very easy as well as fast to switch to a great deal of various other woman on the top sex positions.

1n. Sybian Sex Position

The Sybian sex positions gets its name from the Sybian machine. This is a powerful vibe in a box that you require to straddle in a way quite like the Cowgirl position, with a knee on either side of it on the bed.

Executing the Sybian sex position resembles this, yet is has a number of differences. The initial is that your man will certainly be on either a bed of paddings or a soft-cushioned seat/stool. He will be lying on his back/butt.

The Sybian positions can obtain extremely tedious, really swiftly for your male.

You will need something that your male can comfortably rest on that does not have any type of armrests.

You will still be straddling your guy like in the Cowgirl position, other than instead of hing on your knees on either side of him, you will be on your feet, sitting in his lap while facing him. You can place your hands on your guy or on either side of him to assist keep yourself well balanced.

Girl roles

When in the Sybian placement with your guy, you are going to be utilizing your legs to press yourself up and down on him. You can additionally grind on him gradually by maintaining him inside you and also thrusting forwards as well as in reverse or in a circular activity.

When in the Sybian positions, you are likewise in the perfect positions to place on a show for your man if you such as. This implies that you can start massaging your clitoris as well as breasts. While this feels actually great for you, your male will certainly likewise enjoy it a lot too! When in the Sybian placement you are going to be doing a great deal of the job, but you have the majority of the control additionally, which means that you can lean fairly far forwards or perhaps a little backwards to transform the angle of access.

Male roles

Your guy will certainly be fairly immobile in the Sybian position. If he wants, he can gently thrust back onto you though. Besides that, the most he can do is rub your legs and also waist with his hands as well as keep eye contact with you.

Tips

Finding a soft footstool/seat without armrests is generally the hardest part, although a pile of cushions will certainly do.

You might locate that a Swiss/gym/fitness round will certainly be sufficient.

Just due to the fact that the Sybian sounds hot and not that many individuals have tried it out, do not expect it to offer you way much more fun and pleasure than other positions.

Remarks

You might locate that you invest most of your power just establishing it up as opposed to appreciating it.

1o. Upper Leg Tide Sex Position

The Thigh Tide sex position is an actually fun and simple to do positions. It's best to utilize if you locate that you are getting burnt out from all the routine sex positions with your man.

To do it, your man requires to start by lying on his back with his legs straight and also spread out somewhat apart. He requires to increase one knee somewhat as well as plant his foot on the bed. You after that need to put one knee on either side of his curved leg and also sit down on his crotch while encountering away from him. You after that require to use your legs to raise yourself backwards and forwards on him. Ensure to keep your man's leg to assist stable yourself.

The Thigh Tide positions is fantastic for truly slow, sensuous grinding!
Girl roles
The Thigh Tide position is rather unlike any kind of sex placement that you will have tried previously. Your legs will be doing a lot of the job, pushing on your own up and down on him, however you can keep his leg with your arms to assist draw on your own backwards and forwards.

Among the really trendy aspects of Thigh Tide is that you can bring your clitoris into straight contact with his thigh to boost it as you relocate downwards as well as upwards. If you want to change the angle that your man is entering you at, after that you can lean quite far forwards in the direction of his knee or away, by existing onto his stomach.

Male roles
In the Thigh Tide placement, your male does not need to do a lot. He can simply exist there while you move yourself up and down on him. He can be a lot extra energetic as well.

If he desires, he can simply propelled up and down right into you. As he has one leg curved with a foot on the bed, he will be able to permeate you with a great bit much more force. He can additionally place his hands at the back of your midsection and also press you in the direction of his thigh, to make sure that you get even more clitoral excitement.

By grabbing his knee as well as drawing it in the direction of you, you can get a great deal a lot more clitoral excitement!

Tips
The Thigh Tide is really easy to do, implying that you do not require much versatility in all to do it.

Even though it's an easy placement to do with your man, a lot of pairs still have never ever tried it. This makes it best to utilize if you locate yourselves obtaining burnt out of the normal positions.

Anal sex is equally as very easy as genital sex in the Thigh Tide placement.

Comments

I consider the Thigh Tide position to sort of like a 'Secret Sex Weapon'. For one reason or another it seems that few recognize of it's existence, but once you as well as your man try it, you will enjoy it. You may even want trying it out when encountering in the opposite instructions, while still straddling among his legs.

To examine go to, www.amazon.com/author/tmakopa

Chapter 2. Resting Sex Positions

Why not take a seat as well as allow your guy do the work?

If you have actually tired or sore legs, these resting sex positions are terrific. If you want your guy to do the majority of job, while you literally "kick back and delight in the flight", try out these: Delight Position,. High Chair Position

2a. Delight Sex Position

When you want to be fairly intimate with your guy, the Delight sex position is an excellent one for. It's likewise truly nice because you don't need to put in that much effort to carry out the Delight.

The Delight is truly very easy to do, but very few people have actually tried it.

To set it up, you require to be resting at either the side of your bed or a couch or on the edge of any kind of surface area that is about 12-20 inches from the ground. When you are taking a seat, open your legs vast. Your guy after that kneels before you, encountering you. For him to enter you, you might need to a little lower yourself over the edge. Your male will usually have his legs close together. He can then order your waist or legs as he is thrusting right into you.

Girl roles

When in the Delight placement with your man, you can lean back somewhat (use your arms behind your back to support yourself). You can then gently push on your own towards your man.

When you first try the Delight placement with your guy, you need to try every angle with him, from staying up straight with your arms around his neck to existing right back till you locate an angle that you both actually take pleasure in. If you decide to sit up straight, after that you remain in a best positions to kiss your male, making it much more intimate. The further back you lean though, the less intimate it comes to be.

Guy roles

Your guy has a really very easy task in the Delight position. All he requires to do is simply thrust in and also out. If you as well as leaning back, then he can take his hands off your waist and also utilize them to have fun with your breasts. Aside from that though, this positions is exceptionally easy as well as straightforward for him.

Do not forget to pull your man in close as well as make deep eye contact with him to make it more intimate.

Tips

Getting the height right can often be aggravating. This means seeing to it that your man is high sufficient (or low enough) to make penetration pleasing for both of you. The easy method to fix this elevation issue is by using some firm pillows from your couch.

A variant that you could appreciate is if your guy places his hands under your thighs as well as raises them up. This will certainly aid him to accomplish deeper and more powerful penetration.

If you are not obtaining much clitoral stimulation throughout infiltration, after that do not hesitate to utilize your hands.

Don't ignore eye contact if you intend to make this placement much more intimate!
Remarks
Given your bed/sofa is at the right elevation, then it's uncomplicated to do. Plus if we are both upright, after that it can be rather intimate with our arms around each other and lots of kissing.
2b. High Chair Sex Position

The high chair is a truly enjoyable back access sex placement, where you essentially get to kick back as well as sit, while your man does most of the work. The only point you'll require to execute the High Chair with your male is a bar stool/tall feces.
To establish it up, you are mosting likely to be sitting down on bench stool with your butt hanging around over the edge. So actually you are going to be remaining on the bottom of your thighs, not your butt. Your man will certainly enter you from behind. You can then lean forwards far from your man or in reverse right into your man to find the ideal angle. Obtain him to stand on something company if your man is not high enough to penetrate you.

The High Chair position produces an actually delightful variation on routine Doggy Style.
Do not put anything under your bar feces, see to it gets on a firm, strong surface area to stop any kind of accidents.

Girl roles
When you are in the High Chair placement, you do not have much to do. You really just need to sit there and also allow your man do all the job. You can lean really much onward to the point where your stomach is touching your upper legs. Or you can lean backwards, right into your man for even more affection.
You will certainly be able to masturbate on your own while your man is fucking you if you are not leaning that much ahead.

Man roles
Your man has a quite straightforward work when executing the High Chair with you. He just requires to thrust in as well as out. If you are leaning back into him, then he can wrap his arms around you and even massage therapy your breasts. Your guy must try out penetrating you at different elevations. So he needs to attempt originating from right listed below you to ensure that he is penetrating you quite shallowly. Then he must attempt obtaining higher and higher till you discover something you both delight in.

Tips
- The High Chair is an excellent positions for those that like anal sex.
If your stool does not have a back support, - It works best. If it does have a back support, then you need to face it with one leg on either side of it, so that your male can quickly enter you from behind.

- Remember that you should be remaining on your upper legs (not your butt), so that you butt hangs over the edge of the feces and also enables easy access.

- If you have an interest in maintaining whatever wonderful and tidy, after that placed a towel on the seat before you come down to service.

To examine see, www.amazon.com/author/tmakopa

Chapter 3. Standing Sex Positions

Some of these standing sex positions are excellent for when you intend to have more literally vigorous sex with your male. One more terrific feature of having sex while standing is that you do not need a bed. Perfect for when you want to have sex around the house as well as somewhere else. Ballerina Position, Ben Dover Position, Bodyguard Position, Burning Man Position, Dancer Position, Pump Position, Slow Dance Position, Washing Machine Position

3a. Ballerina Sex Position

The Ballerina sex position is one of those actually unique ones that 95% of women will certainly just never have the ability to execute. This is merely to the issue of flexibility. Nevertheless if you can perform it, after that it can be both very intimate and enjoyable.

As you can see aware above, carrying out the ballerina is difficult without a great deal of flexibility.

To pull the Ballerina off, you both require to start by encountering each other while standing. You are after that mosting likely to need to elevate one leg upwards until you are resting it on your guy's shoulder, while balancing on your other leg. Your leg that is hing on your man's shoulder is going to be practically directly, allowing you to be really close to your male.

Lady roles

When performing the Ballerina with your male, you're initial work is to get comfy.

Keep in mind If you are not adaptable sufficient, after that you will undoubtedly be in pain when doing it.

You need to invest most of your time staying well balanced on one leg which you require to maintain straight, while enabling your guy to do the remainder of the job. When accepting you which will certainly place a great deal of extra stress on your leg, you additionally require to make sure that your guy doesn't squeeze you as well hard.

Male roles

Your man is going to be doing all the thrusting in the Ballerina. He needs to initially set you up in position with among your legs over his shoulder and also make sure that you are not in any kind of discomfort prior to he enters you. When he does enter you, he needs to start out by just really delicately embedding as well as out.

Again, your comfort is the most important thing (especially the first time you try it), so your man needs to take things really slowly. He will need to bend his knees a little and thrust up into you if he is taller than you. He can additionally cover his hands around your back and also pull you in delicately in the direction of him with each thrust.

Tips

When you are lying down on your back, - A great way to first test the Ballerina with your man is to try it. By doing this you do not have to fret about keeping well balanced.

- When executing the Ballerina, your male can try propelling his penis deep inside you and after that keep it there while scrubing his pubic bone up and down your clitoris.

- If you are very flexible and very small, your guy can raise you up and hold you near to him while thrusting in and also out.

Remarks

Without a doubt the Ballerina is possibly among one of the most unique and also 'around' positions that you can do with your man Just because it's more exotic and out there doesn't necessarily mean that it's better. Don't break your leg trying to perform the Ballerina with your man.

3b. Ben Dover Sex Position

Ben Dover: You need to lean forward & equilibrium with your hands, while your man holds you from behind

The Ben Dover sex positions is an incredibly enjoyable back entrance placement that you must attempt if you already like Doggy Style or the Basset Hound. You need a little versatility as well as a bit of leg toughness to perform it well.

To begin doing the Bed Dover, your both need to deal with in the same direction while standing upright. Your man then requires to enter you. You then need to lean over and stretch you arms out until you are touching the floor with them to balance yourself when he has penetrated you. Preferably, you should try to maintain you hands as near your feet as possible, but if you are not that versatile or it feels awkward, then feel free to lean onward a little bit.

Girl roles

When you initially start doing the Ben Dover sex positions, you may find it to be a little disorientating. This is because your head will be upside-down, so ensure to inform your man to go easy and slow initially. Then once you obtain comfortable, begin to use your arms to push back onto your male. If your hands are located right by your feet, then you won't be able to push back that much.

You can additionally try taking him deep and after that keeping him there while you grind backwards and forwards on him utilizing your hips.

Guy roles

When your male remains in the Ben Dover positions, all he needs to do is just thrust in and also out. He can likewise bend his knees and also lean back to change his angle of access. He can obviously take all this up a notch also. He can likewise put his hands on your waist to assist regulate exactly how rapid and deep he is permeating you. Or if you are searching for something a little more kinky, after that he can order you by the hair for a somewhat rougher time. A really pleasurable point that your male can do in the Ben Dover is to propelled deep inside you. While staying inside you, he can after that grind himself right up and down you by flexing his knees. This is excellent for altering points up instead of just thrusting in as well as out.

Tips

You will burn out much quicker than your guy will certainly when in the Ben Dover. If you locate your arms beginning to count on jelly, after that try flexing your knees a little.

You will certainly discover that you can lean back rather greatly right into your man, which will take a lot of the weight off your arms. This is an additional fantastic way to give your arms a remainder.

Your male can use his hand(s) to give some hand-operated stimulation to your clitoris as well as around your vaginal canal.

The Ben Dover is perfect for anal sex as well.

- Your male needs to maintain explore his angle of entrance until he discovers something that you truly appreciate.

Ben Dover: He can thrust forwards & pull you in at the same time in this positions for much more intense sex.

Remarks

Occasionally doing it up against a wall surface is a wonderful as it indicates you can quickly press yourself back to your male

3c. Bodyguard Sex Position

The Bodyguard sex positions resembles a cross in between routine Spooning as well as the Ben Dover placement. It's wonderful for couples who want the naughtiness of Doggy style with the affection of Spooning.

The Bodyguard position is very comparable to the Tea spooning position.
To carry out the Bodyguard with your man, you both require to stand upright, encountering parallel. Your guy will be behind you and will enter you. He will usually need to bend his knees to penetrate you if he's taller than you. From here, it's simply an easy case of him thrusting in and also out or you pushing yourself back onto him.

Lady roles
It's completely up to you how involved you want to be when you are in the Bodyguard position. If you desire your male to take control as well as do all the work, that's penalty. But if you intend to obtain included too, then there is a series of points you can do.
One is pressing yourself back onto your man as he fucks you. You can additionally cover your arms in reverse around his midsection and butt and also pull him right into you as he is thrusting. A very intimate point that you can do in the Bodyguard positions is to lean your head backwards to make sure that it is kind of hing on his shoulder which will certainly enable him to kiss you on the cheek as well as neck.

Guy roles
Unlike some of the various other positions s, the Bodyguard is truly straightforward to do. All your guy requires to do is merely thrust forwards and also backwards. By correcting his legs to get greater or bending them as well as getting lower, he can transform his angle of entrance.
As your male is located behind you, he can wrap his arms around you as well as hold you closer to make it extra intimate. He can literally get you anywhere, around the waist, the shoulders or perhaps the neck. He will likewise locate that holding onto your midsection permits him to more powerfully penetrate you with each thrust.

Tips
If you like this position, but want to transform it up a bit after that get your man to flex his knees to obtain somewhat below you as well as propelled up into you rather than just thrusting flat.
If you wish to offer a different sensation and more friction for your man, after that bring your legs close together.

For optimal get in touch with, see to it that your male totally wraps his arms around you (either by putting his arms under your arms and grabbing your shoulders or by placing 1 arm around your top body as well as 1 around your lower body.

Try leaning right back into your male as well as let gravity do all the job to ensure that you do not need to returned in him.

Remarks

The Bodyguard placement allows you to be truly close and also intimate with your enthusiast. When you are in this position, it's also really easy to switch from slow passionate sex to vigorous and rough sex in a second.

3d. Burning Man Sex Position

The Burning Man sex position gets it's name from the truth that you can have some really enthusiastic, fiery, 'burning' sex with your man in this position. To do it, you need either a counter top or table.

You need to encounter the counter top and then lay your stomach over it while maintaining your feet on the ground. Your guy can then permeate you from behind either vaginally or anally. As your legs stay on the ground, they will certainly function as an anchor, maintaining you in place to ensure that your guy can really offer you some hard, extreme infiltration without you slipping out of place.

Woman roles
When you are in the Burning Man position, you are going to be fairly easy. You put your hands on it and push yourself back onto your man if there is a wall in front of you.
One more point you can do to raise the enthusiasm, is to reverse and also make eye contact with your guy while he is propelling right into you. You can use your hand (or hands) to masturbate yourself to increase your chances of cumming if you're having anal sex with your man.
You can additionally obtain a bit much more upright in this positions as well as lean your upper body back in the direction of him while in the Burning Man to ensure that it really feels more like the Bodyguard position and includes a bit of affection. He will be able to wrap his hands around your waist and shoulders when you are upright and have your back against his stomach.

Male roles
Your male will be doing the bulk of the work in the Burning Man. All he has to concentrate on is simply thrusting in and out if it's his first time trying it. He additionally has the alternative of holding onto your midsection or shoulders to draw you into him as he is propelling.
If he likes to feel dominant when making love with you, then he can grab hold of your hair.
If he wants to make it more sensual and intimate then instead of pulling you upright, he can lean over your back, so it feels like he is spooning you over the counter.

Your male can grab your shoulders and also draw you in for stronger, much deeper propelling.

Woman roles

Make sure that your male isn't also forceful in this position. Your body won't move as much when he thrusts into you because you are wedged up against a counter top or table. This suggests that he is more likely to unintentionally harm you by thrusting also hard. So inform him if he is!

This can create some truly kinky, unexpected sex when you are in the kitchen or living space. All your man has to do is lift it up and pull down your panties if you are wearing a skirt. Points such as this make a welcome adjustment from only ever before making love in the bedroom.

Your male is entirely totally free to move around you in this positions, so obtain him to experiment with different angles up until you discover one that you both appreciate.

Remarks

If having anal sex), it's very flexible and one of the great things about it is that your man can easily provide some extra pleasure using his fingers (especially.

3e. Dancer Sex Position

The Dancer sex position is a very intimate one, but requires a little of leg strength to correctly pull it off. In a great deal of methods the Dancer is very comparable to the Ballerina sex position, yet does not need as much adaptability.

To execute the Dancer, you both require to begin by standing upright as well as dealing with each other. You require to raise among your legs and then wrap it around your man. You can wrap it around your man's waist if you are strong and flexible enough. If you can't raise it up that high, then you can wrap it around the back of his thigh.

You don't have to raise your upper hand very high in the Dancer position.

With your leg twisted around your male, he then enters you and also begins propelling right into you. Your man can aid you remain in position by wrapping one hand around your waistline and also holding your other leg with his hand/arm.

Lady roles

If you find your leg getting tired, then simply switch over legs!

You'll discover the Dancer positions to be extremely intimate for both you and your man. You can look him right in the eyes and hold each other really carefully. To add to the intimacy, attempt wrapping your hands around his waistline. Even far better though, is to place them under his arms as well as order him by his back/shoulders.

You'll locate that with your leg twisted around his midsection you can draw yourself right into your man, yet this gets strenuous pretty quickly. Besides that, you will find that you use up a great deal of power just keeping your balance on 1 leg.

Male roles

Your male will certainly be making use of one arm to hold you close, while using his various other arm to help maintain your leg increased and also wrapped around him. He will be doing all the propelling. He can relocate his hips back and forth, thrusting flat, but this can knock you off balance. A better means for him to drive, so that it's less complicated for you to maintain your equilibrium is to flex his knees for more vertical propelling.

Tips

You will discover it much easier to stand as well as keep your balance when depending on your entire foot, not just your toes, so make certain you inform your man to spread his legs and also bend his knees to come to your degree, as opposed to 'raising' you up.

If you are not made use of to this placement, after that you'll locate that you can only hold it for a minute or 2.

Don't neglect that you can change which leg you are basing on if you are getting tired.

Comments

I find the Dancer position to be excellent to attempt once or twice, yet it's definitely not one of my favorites (I do not entirely hate it though!). A slight variant that I such as to attempt is to both be on one foot, both covering our other leg around each other. If you like it, try it yourself and also see!

3f. Pump Sex Position

The Pump is a terrific sex position that is a variation of Doggy Style. As you can probably imagine from a name like Pump, your male will actually be pumping you from behind.

The Pump is terrific for around your home, any place you have a couch or durable chair.

To get into the Pump placement, you require to begin by positioning on your own on something like a sofa or chair with your legs slightly curved. Your guy will certainly after that enter you from behind while also standing. The Pump is excellent for either anal sex or normal genital sex with your man. You can after that put your arms in front of you onto the wall or your elbow joints to hold you in place as well as push back versus your guy.

Girl roles

When in the Pump position, your male is most definitely the one in charge, which is ideal if you favor for your guy to take control during sex. You can additionally push back versus him if you desire deeper and also more powerful infiltration from him. You can spread your arms out and relax your upper body against the wall surface.

You will certainly discover that by angling your body, bending your knees and changing your position, you will eventually discover a position that you really enjoy and also obtain a lot of pleasure out of. You can also put your hands behind you to get onto your guy and assistance to draw him in towards you.

In some cases your male can get a little carried away when penetrating you in the Pump. So see to it to allow him understand if he is.

Male roles

Your man has a really very easy task in the Pump placement. It mainly contains him just thrusting in as well as out. If he is devoted to having fantastic sex, after that he ought to constantly be trying out with exactly how much he pulls you out in the direction of him and his angle of access so that you both get as much satisfaction from the Pump as feasible.

Your man also shouldn't forget about his hands. He can wrap them around your waist while thrusting into you. Or around your shoulders. If you enjoy playing submissive as well as dominant throughout sex, then he can even put his hand around your throat. But see to it to review this with him in advance.

Tips

When you like your male to be in control, - The Pump is a terrific placement for.

- But at the same time, the pump can feel like Spooning while standing up with your man which feels a lot more sensuous as well as caring.

- Your male remains in an excellent placement to reach about as well as start rubbing you simply outside your vagina when in the Pump placement.

Comments
The Pump sex position is great. It's best for every little thing from romantic and also sluggish sex to much quicker, enthusiastic sex with your man.

3g. Slow Dance Sex Position

The Slow Dance sex positions is a truly fun placement for you as well as your guy where you are both standing up. Luckily it's not virtually as challenging to perform the Ballerina or Dancer positions.

To execute the Slow Dance with your man, you both require to be standing while dealing with each other. If your male is taller than you, after that he requires to bend his knees as well as obtain a little lower than you to ensure that he can enter you. To help him enter you, you'll need to open your legs a little bit. You simply need to wrap your arms around each other as well as your male can propelled up right into you.

The Slow Dance setting is terrific for slow intimate sex, while standing.

Then the Slow Dance will certainly be impossible to perform unless you are standing on a stairs, if you are much smaller sized than your guy. If you are taller than him, then you can bend your knees and reduced on your own on him.

Girl roles

Relocating from the Slow Dance to the Carry & stand positions is really very easy.

When in the Slow Dance placement, you can move up as well as down with your guy as he drives right into you to make it a rhythmic movement. But if you want much more enthusiastic sex, then you can thrust back against your man with each of his drives.

If you wish to make the sex more intimate as well as romantic, then you ought to simply try grinding on him, by keeping him deep inside you, while you move up and also down on him making use of both your legs and hips.

Male roles

The Slow Dance is easy and also actually uncomplicated for your guy. He simply needs to go up and down utilizing his legs. As covering his arms around your midsection, he can put them under your butt to draw you in with each drive. He can additionally place his hands under your arms and also get your shoulders to assist him permeate you with a bit more force.

Tips

If you are having slow-moving sensuous sex in the Slow Dance placement with your man, it can be really sexy to maintain eye contact with him. However if you have actually just begun dating or it's your first time making love with each other, after that it may really feel a little bit too intense for him.

Something a lot of individuals like when you carefully run your hand through over their head, delicately massaging his scalp with your fingers. The Slow Dance is ideal for this.

Remarks

I really see the Slow Dance as a very intimate positions. While you can most definitely go quite rapid and have enthusiastic sex throughout the Slow Dance, you may find that you really obtain a whole lot more from it by slowing points down as well as taking your time with it. You are in the best placement to hold each other firmly, to look each other in the eye as well as kiss each other during it.

3h. Washing Machine Sex Position

The Washing Machine sex position is the one position in which you definitely have to have one details tool ... a washing equipment.

The actually trendy aspect of washing devices is that they are never ever in the bedroom definition that you require to make use of a different area in your residence to make love in which is way much more interesting!

When you have located a cleaning maker, placed some washes inside it as well as turn it on a high spin positions. Following you require to lean over it while still standing, just like in the Burning Man placement. This will help to bring your groin area in closer contact with the shaking cleaning equipment. Your male will certainly after that enter you from behind and begin thrusting right into you while standing.

Here you can see our pair showing the Washing Machine. Your guy can order your hands much like aware to draw you in to him with each drive.

Girl roles

The Washing Machine placement is one in which your guy has to take control and be dominant, while you just require to loosen up, release and enjoy on your own. If you want, you can be fairly active as well.

Many cleaning machines are beside a wall surface, so you can place your distribute in front of you on the wall surface and also push back against your man as he is thrusting right into you for more powerful infiltration. You can likewise stand up to make sure that you are more upright, like in the Bodyguard Position and reach behind to begin rubbing you guy.

Male roles

Your man requires to do most of the work in the Washing Machine placement. He will certainly be propelling while standing upright. If you are leaning right over the washing maker, your man can lean on top of you to make it a lot more intimate.

The Washing Machine placement is ideal for both rectal and vaginal sex. If you are having rectal sex with your man, then he can get to about as well as beginning fingering you or just scrubing your clit to assist you orgasm. If he intends to thrust deeper into you, after that your guy can get your waist/hips with his hands and pull you right into him. If he intends to thrust even harder, then he can order your shoulders.

Tips

You'll get the best vibrations from your cleaning machine when it's spinning fastest (which is generally in the direction of the end before the washing equipment transforms itself off).

Try utilizing a vibrator to add additional enjoyment!

Make sure to let your male understand if he is getting carried away. It has actually been understood to happen!

Remarks

The Washing Machine is not purely a sex position. It's even more of a sex concept or sex pointer. Keeping that being stated, it still really feels fantastic and also is a terrific method to flavor points up if you discover that your sex life is growing dull.

To evaluate browse through, www.amazon.com/author/tmakopa

Chapter 4. Unique Sex Positions

If you find yourself getting tired with the 'Regular' sex positions, after that try a few of the se exotic ones! All of the se exotic sex positions are fairly hard to categorize, so I determined to give them a section to themselves as they are either a lot different from the various other sex placement groups or they are really tough to carry out. If you ever want to try something significantly various, then I highly suggest that you try out one of the se. You might want to stretch first: Acrobat Position, Betty Rocker Position, Big Dipper Position, Bridge Position, Chair Riding Position, G Spot Sniper Position, Jellyfish Position, Lazy Wheelbarrow Position, Life Raft Position, Little Dipper Position, Octopus Position, Pearly Gates Position, Pile driver Position, Piston Position, Scissors Position, Socket Position, Stand & Carry Position, Swiss Miss Position, Tango Position, Wheel Barrow Position

4a. Acrobat Sex Position

The Acrobat sex placement is a variant of the reverse cowgirl positions. The acrobat is a fantastic position that leaves you really feeling exposed, with your man in control, while also providing a lot of G-Spot stimulation.

To perform it your guy pushes his back, you after that require to get involved in the reverse cowgirl sex position on top of him. This implies that you require to straddle him, encountering away from him, to ensure that he is looking at your back. You will be on your knees. You need to then lay back onto your male, while attempting to keep your knees on the bed.

You will find that the Acrobat gets tiring very quickly if you are not that flexible.

Keeping your knees on the bed is not always possible, yet do attempt. Your guy can place his hands on your back and also slowly reduce you down.

Lady roles

You will be quite immobile when you are in the Acrobat sex position. Simply put, you will find it tough to do much besides gyrate your hips onto your man. Relying on what your male is doing, you may require to use one hand to steady on your own on top of him.

You are in a great position to masturbate on your own when doing the acrobat or place your arms back and about your guy.

Guy roles

Your male will certainly be doing a good deal of the operate in the Acrobat position. He needs to be helping to hold you in place and also propelling into you from listed below. He's additionally in a fantastic position to rub your clit or finger you if you are having anal sex. He can likewise use his hands to gently massage your busts. He will providing a lot of direct simulation to your G-Spot if your man thrusts up and down.

Your man can grab your shoulders and pull you down with each thrust if you like to have quite intense sex in this position.

Tips

- This position is fantastic to make use of when having anal sex with your man. Because it's a position that allows your man to finger you at the same time, it's also great.

- Ideally when you are performing the Acrobat, you ought to have your knees on the bed. Nevertheless many people aren't that versatile and also discover this positions unpleasant. This is why I advise that you lift them up as you lean back so that you are constantly comfortable and do not constrain.

When performing the Acrobat, - Your man is in the perfect position to kiss you on your neck and back.

Remarks

I locate that this can be a fantastic positions for your guy to take a lot of control throughout sex (even though you are on top). If you like him being really dominant, while you feel exposed as well as submissive, after that you'll like this. He can even put his hand around your neck for that extra feeling of dominance if you like.

4b. Betty Rocker Sex Position

The Betty Rocker sex position is one that a lot of pairs never ever also attempt. It may look a little 'available' or unique, yet it's actually really simple to execute.

Your male needs to exist flat on the bed with his legs just a little bit apart. You then require to straddle him, however instead of facing him, reverse, to ensure that he is now considering your back. While upright, slide his penis inside you, to ensure that you are currently in the Asian Cowgirl placement with him. Start to lean forwards slowly and rest part of your weight on your arms or his legs once he is inside you.

Remember to start slowly in the Betty Rocker position so that you do not inadvertently harm your guy!

Currently you can start shaking forwards and backwards on your legs and arms. The name Betty Rocker. The fun doesn't stop there. If rocking doesn't do it for you, you can also move yourself up and down on your man's penis or he can thrust into you.

Girl roles

When in the Betty Rocker placement, you have a variety of selections. You can simply gradually rock forwards as well as in reverse on your guy.

Simply be really mindful not to rock as well far forwards, as you can injure your man by placing way too much strain on his suspensory ligaments.

Or you can bounce up and down on him. One more option is to gradually gyrate your hips as well as midsection while he remains deep inside you to force his penis right around the within walls of your vagina.

Guy roles

Your guy can simply lie there and also delight in the view of your bum as well as back. If he intends to take a more active function, after that he can thrust up and down. He can thrust up into you and fuck you really fast if you keep stationary while holding your own weight above your man. Or you can sink down onto his lap for slower yet deeper and also tougher infiltration. If your guy's midsection and legs begin to burn out, then he can get your bum and also force you backwards and forwards on his dick, with you supplying just a little assistance. Be careful that he doesn't get you also hard, unless you like rough sex.

If you like it, your man can spank your bum, while you are in this position.

Tips

If your man's penis is not that adaptable, then you will certainly be a lot more upright (possibly with your hands on your upper legs), making it look a whole lot more like Asian Cowgirl than like Betty Rocker.

A great deal of pairs consider this to be a hot, exotic and dirty sex placement, while not viewing as that intimate.

Remarks

As a great deal of couples have not tried it, it's great to present into the room to spice things up. It's particularly excellent if you want to have a 'hot' sex session in contrast to an intimate one.

4c. Big Dipper Sex Position

The Big Dipper sex position is more a marathon than an incredibly enjoyable placement like Missionary or the Coital Alignment Technique (CAT). It's a sex positions that I think about more like sexercise than sex. A great deal of individuals see it as more of a novelty positions as opposed to a major sexual position.

As you can see in the picture, carrying out the Big Dipper is really exhausting for your male.

To perform the Big Dipper, you need to set up a strong chair facing a bed or sofa. Your male requires to place himself with the chiar simply behind him, so if he tried to sit down, he would certainly just miss out on the chair and also would certainly fall on the floor. He after that needs to put his hands on the chair behind him. Next he requires to rest his feet on a sofa/bed ahead on him. His whole body will certainly currently rise. He must currently resemble he will perform a tricep bench dip (a workout for the health club).

You then require to straddle him while facing him, away any of your weight on him. Your man will after that use his arms to reduced himself and after that push himself up right into you.

It's extremely essential that your male flexes his knees a little the whole time he is carrying out the Big Dipper to avoid any type of injuries from happening.

Lady roles

You may feel like just staying there and not doing a whole lot when you are having sex in the Big Dipper position. That's fine, but your guy will certainly be exhausted within regarding 40 secs.

If you want to be more active and for sex to last longer in this placement, then you can begin crouching backwards and forwards on your man, while he stays still. This will enable you to sex in this positions for a little bit much longer. You can additionally grind on him as opposed to simply bowing up and down. Simply make sure not to relax your weight on him as it's really unpleasant to be in this placement.

Male roles

Your man is primarily going to be doing the tricep bench dip workout while propelling into you. This indicates that he is going to lower himself as well as elevate himself using just his hands. This will rapidly tire your male's arms to fatigue.

A far better method is for your male to maintain his arms extended straight with only a mild bend in them while utilizing his hips to thrust into you, while you continue to be in position above him. He should have the ability to do this for a bit much longer (generally 2-3 mins) than rising and also down utilizing only his arms.

Tips

- Most feel that Big Dipper is an uniqueness position, worth trying as soon as for enjoyable, however not worth using frequently with your guy.

If you are serious about it, - You should experiment with variations of the Big Dipper. Try it backwards. Or finding out forwards. Or in reverse. Locate what jobs best for you.

- If your guy is battling staying on his hands and also pressing himself up and down, he must try resting on his elbow joints and thrusting with his hips instead.

Thoughts

I actually see the Big Dipper as a novelty position, that's fun to attempt if you are goofing around with your man. Other than that, I wouldn't recommend it ever.

4d. Bridge Sex Position

You might find that the Bridge sex placement falls more right into the category of Sexercise or perhaps a novelty sex placement than super-pleasurable sex. This is due to the fact that it's quite difficult for you to execute for greater than a minute or 2.

To carry out the Bridge, you require to get involved in the 'crab' position that is used in acrobatics. This suggests that you will get on all fours, other than that your back will certainly be encountering the ground/bed. Your male now requires to get onto his knees between your legs while encountering you. He then enters you and places his hand on your thighs to help draw you in the direction of him with each thrust.

As you can see, the Bridge position is quite arduous. However it is a really enjoyable position to try at least when.

Just maintaining on your own boosted in this placement is extremely exhausting.

Woman roles

When in the Bridge placement, you will regrettably be spending the majority of your time trying to maintain your equilibrium, which does not leave a lot of time to appreciate on your own.

If you are strong enough, after that you can gradually propelled against your male as he enters you, yet other than that you must concentrate on placing your hands and also feet in one of the most comfortable positions you can find.

Man roles

Your man firstly needs to understand exactly how uneasy the Bridge can be for you. When he begins making love with you, he requires to go slowly so as not to hurt you, knock you off balance or place excessive strain on your shoulders.

He must delicately embedded as well as out. After that once you are both comfy, he can grab your waistline or upper legs as well as start pulling you in towards him with each thrust. Instead of thrusting in an out, your guy can pull you in towards him fairly strongly and afterwards grind his pubic read up and down your clit as well as clitoral hood. Your man will certainly be then in a setting where he can additionally massage therapy and rub your busts with his hands while carrying out the Bridge.

Tips

This is a really exhausting placement for your arms as well as shoulders. Even 30 secs is excessive for some.

One of the excellent things about the Bridge is the feeling of being exposed as well as really feeling rather at risk, especially if you curve your back.

Resting on your elbow joints as opposed to your hands will certainly enable you to do it for much longer. Most people just attempted the Bridge once or twice and after that ignored it. It was way too much benefit only a percentage of enjoyment.

Remarks

Even though it is somewhere between a novelty setting as well as Sexercise setting, it's still a wonderful placement to make use of with your male just for the benefit of keeping things fun and fascinating in the bedroom.

4e. Chair Riding Sex Position

The Chair Riding sex position can be considered a relatively unique one. As you can possibly think of, the Chair Riding position needs you to utilize 2 chairs to do it. If you don't make use of the best chairs for this setting, you might discover it to be rather unpleasant.

Getting set up in the Chair Riding placement takes longer than the remainder of the sex positions in guide.

To set up this placement, initially get 2 chairs to make sure that they are facing each other. They should be fairly close together so that they are practically touching each other. Your man then needs to muffle one and open his legs fairly large. You after that need to muffle the various other with your legs close together. You will certainly both be facing each other for this setting. Currently you need to slowly bring yourself in the direction of his penis while he brings his penis closer to your vaginal canal. You will discover that raising your legs upwards makes it a lot easier. When doing the Octopus placement makes it a great deal more comfy for you, you might also find that placing your ankles over his shoulders like you would certainly. Your guy can after that keep your legs or order your arms to delicately thrust into you.

Woman roles

Your major goal is in fact to discover a comfortable position when you are in the Chair Riding setting. If you are using wooden chairs, you in fact may discover it to be too awkward to enjoy the sex.

You can carefully grind on your male or raise your body up and down. You will be slightly stooped over the entire time you are in the Chair Riding placement which will permit you to easily masturbate yourself. Apart from that, there is actually not a lot you can do in this position.

Guy roles

When your man is in the Chair Riding position, he will certainly have his legs open wide, with his feet either on the flooring or on the edges of your chair. He also needs to try as well as discover a comfortable position for himself so that the chair does not go into his back too much. To propelled into you, he can order you by your thighs or by your arms and gently pull you in towards him. Simply ensure he doesn't pull as well hard, or else he can hurt your arms/legs. Your guy can drop his hand are massage your clit, however other than that, there is not a great deal he can do.

Tips

- Chair option is necessary. You are both in for an uneasy time if you pick the wrong chairs. You need a little adaptability for this set, especially if you plan on increasing your legs over your male's shoulders.

4f. G-Spot Sniper Sex Position

The G-Spot Sniper position looks truly unusual when you first try it. But stay with it. It's a wonderful placement if you wish to get some significant G-Spot excitement from your guy

Try locking your feet with each other behind your man's neck to assist raise your reduced body off the bed. Your guy can assist keep you elevated using his hands under your midsection.

To get into the G-Spot Sniper setting, you need to start off having sex with your guy like you would certainly in the Deep Impact sex position. This means that you require to push your back on the bed with your legs airborne, directing at the ceiling. Your male will certainly be permeating you while on his knees. Yet as opposed to spreading his knees apart to lower himself down in the direction of you like in a number of the various other sex positions I teach, he requires to maintain his knees with each other so that his is as high as possible.

He will certainly require to get you by your knees/legs as well as draw you up towards him to make sure that he can permeate you. Practically your entire body will now be pointing in the direction of the ceiling and also you will carry every one of your weight on your

shoulders/upper back while keeping your males legs to steady yourself.
Don't try the G Spot Sniper placement if you have a negative back.

Lady roles
Entering the G Spot Sniper setting is your very first task. Starting from a setting like the Launch Pad will make every little thing simpler and even more natural. It can really feel a little unpleasant as well as awkward, but just power through it due to the fact that the sex will certainly be worth it. The sensation of being upside down with your guy will certainly additionally feel a little odd at. You'll locate that after being in this setting a couple of times it's not a big deal and also you'll obtain used to it.

You just have 2 tasks in the G-Spot Sniper position:
1) Stay comfy without hurting your back.
2) Staying in setting so that your guy can continually penetrate you. Hanging on to his leg will maintain you ready.

Male roles
Your man needs to hold you ready. While getting your upper legs, he can very easily hurt you by extending your skin. So he needs to be really careful to ensure he is soft with you. Afterwards, he simply requires to focus on embedding and out.

If you like tougher, much more passionate as well as even animalistic sex, after that your guy can really pound you hard by drawing you right into him with each drive. He can additionally use one hand to hold both of your legs, while using his freedom to scrub your clitoris.

Try differing exactly how high you elevate your waist off the bed till you struck the 'sweet spot'.

Tips
When done right, the G-Spot Sniper can lead to some really powerful G- Spot climaxes. Yet to get it right, your man will require to attempt changing his angle of access a few times up until he discovers an angle that you like.
You can try anal sex with the G-Spot Sniper placement, however many people much favor genital sex in this placement.
When you are both trying this placement for the first time, it can be quite uncomfortable and also 'fumbly' to point your body towards the ceiling. There is absolutely nothing you can do about this, so attempt not to fret. As soon as you are both in position, you'll see (as well as feel) that it was totally worth it!
Comments
It feels wonderful really enjoyed it even though it looks unpleasant. I extremely recommend that you try it with your man

4g. Jellyfish Sex Position

The Jellyfish placement is quite tough to do. You and your male both require to have a little of strength and also great equilibrium to do it for any length of time. But it does feel very intimate which can make it totally worth it ultimately.

The Jellyfish is rather a challenging setting to do. Yet it is great to try if you find yourself getting burnt out of all the other sex positions.

Your man starts by stooping in the middle of the bed, with his butt hing on his calves/ankles while keeping his top body upright and straight. You then require to straddle him and squat down on him to make sure that he enters you. You both after that need to wrap your arms around each other. Neither of you will be propelling that much. When carrying out the Jellyfish, you will certainly spend most of your time doing a grinding activity, back and forth onto each other.

Girl roles

As you are bowing over your male, you'll discover that you have a lot of the control over exactly how deep and also quick your man enters you. If you like, you can squat backwards and forwards on your male. You'll discover that this obtains tiring rather quick as well as feels extra like Sexercise.

As you are holding each other snugly, you remain in the best setting to kiss his neck and ears, but you'll find maintaining your balance while kissing him on the lips to be a whole lot harder.

Man roles

As you get on top of your male and also he will certainly get on his knees, he will certainly find it truly tough to do anything at all when doing the Jellyfish with you. He can put his arms around you also as well as kiss you on the neck and also ears as well, but mainly your male is simply going to be focusing on helping you to maintain your balance.

Tips

- It's a setting that's actually hard to do for a long period of time. If you are interested in doing an exercise while making love with your man (Sexercise) after that it's wonderful, but if you wish to actually enjoy yourself with your man and don't want to fret about getting aches, attempt a different sex setting.

- A good idea concerning the Jellyfish setting is that you are close to your male, which at least makes it intimate.

4h. Lazy Wheelbarrow Sex Position

The Lazy Wheelbarrow sex setting is anything however careless! To perform it requires a good deal of effort.

Performing the Lazy Wheelbarrow can really feel a little awkward.

To do the Lazy Wheelbarrow with your male, he requires to begin by sitting down on a chair or a sofa (without any armrests) with his legs with each other. You then need to sit down on him with your legs together like you would certainly in the Lap Dance or Back Seat Driver positions. You after that require to lean forward, as far as feasible as well as put your hands on the ground in front of you. Your tummy will certainly be hing on your thighs.

Girl roles

Because you will remain in a really awkward setting when performing the Lazy Wheelbarrow, you won't be able to do much besides attempting to maintain yourself comfy as well as using your arms to maintain yourself up.

There are a lot of points that you as well as your guy will be performing in the Lazy Wheelbarrow position that you may not have done in the past, so make certain to let your man recognize if he is doing anything that harms or is uncomfortable.

Man roles

Your man's first objective is making sure you are not too uncomfortable and that he is carry enough of your weight when you are getting into the Lazy Wheelbarrow position.

As he is taking a seat, he will certainly discover it challenging to propelled right into you. Instead you will certainly be grinding on each other. Your man needs to gently move you forward and backwards over him by holding onto your waist.

Tips

- Just due to the fact that the Lazy Wheelbarrow is exotic, 'out there' or is difficult to carry out does not indicate it's better. You'll locate that they are great deals of positions that are way a lot more gratifying, pleasurable and also simpler to do than the Lazy Wheelbarrow.

- If you like lots of propelling throughout sex, after that you'll hate the Lazy Wheelbarrow. It's really challenging for your guy to do any type of thrusting during it whatsoever.

4i. Life Raft Sex Position

The Life Raft sex placement might initially seem like a novelty sex placement for you and also your guy. It's actually quite pleasurable for a ton of reasons.

To get into the Life Raft position, you are mosting likely to need one of those inflatable pool bed mattress that you can push. Some call these 'lilos', others call them inflatable swimming pool beds. You then require lie on your belly on the mattress in a swimming pool, with your vagina in the middle of the bed mattress, while in shallow water.

Here is the Life Raft showed on a table

Your man after that straddles you, with his feet on the bottom of the swimming pool to make sure that he is not resting on you, pressing you downwards, however instead towering above you. He then enters you and begins thrusting.

Woman roles

When you are in the Life Raft setting, you don't need to do anything. What you'll be doing is making sure that you fit which your vagina is constantly out of the water.

Why? Water (as well as specifically chlorinated water) tends to dry out your vaginal area as well as removes your all-natural lubrication quicker than you can generate it. Because there is too much friction and not enough lubrication, this means that your vagina will start to become painful. Keeping it out of the water is not easy. You may locate that it's simpler to just have some lubrication with you and also to utilize that to maintain yourself wet throughout sex. That, just lie there and enjoy the ride!

Man roles

Your male does not have a specifically difficult work either. He just needs to embeded an out while holding you in position. This means that he needs to hold onto either your midsection or shoulders or even your hair.

He also requires to make certain that he doesn't push you down right into the water too much either as this will have your vaginal canal continuously in the water and also drying out. So besides embedding as well as out, your male's main job is making sure that you are comfortable.

Tips

Don't limit yourself to simply resting on your tummy. Check out the Life Raft while in various other positions like lying on your back with your legs over the side or on your back with your legs in the air.

Make certain you do not break any laws when executing the Life Raft with your man.

Try the Life Raft with your male relaxing while you straddle him in, in a position comparable to Cowgirl.

Remarks

I am a big follower of the Life Raft. This is principally since it's so various to most various other sex setting that you will ever before likely take part in with your man along with the fact that it's really versatile.

4j. Little Dipper Sex Position

The Little Dipper sex position is really just an uniqueness placement that is far more about Sexercise than it is about having terrific sex. The Little Dipper is significantly the little sibling of the Big Dipper setting.

Executing the Little Dipper calls for a good bit of stamina. You can save energy by resting down on your man's lap and letting him do the thrusting.

To establish the Little Dipper setting, you need a bed/sofa and also a durable chair/footstool. Your man requires to rest on the flooring on his back in between the bed as well as footstool. You are then mosting likely to place yourself over him and sit down on his crotch. You need to after that position your feet on the stool and also your hands behind you on the bed. You are after that going to lift yourself backwards and forwards on your man using your arms like your would certainly if your were executing bench dips in the fitness center.

Woman roles

In the Little Dipper setting, all you are going to do is simply increase yourself backwards and forwards in addition to your male using your arms.

Like I've already said, the Little Dipper is a novelty position, so you will certainly find that you will only have the ability to last 10-- 60 secs in this position before your arms rely on jelly as well as you cannot raise on your own up any more. When you cannot lift on your own up on your male anymore, attempt simply muffling him and also grinding instead to give your arms a remainder.

An alternate way to carry out the Little Dipper that will permit you to last a little bit longer is to just hold yourself in position, while your guy embed and also out.

Male roles

Your man will not be doing much in the Little Dipper placement. He can thrust up and down into you if you are holding yourself still. Or if you are grinding on him, after that he can use his hands to offer you some clitoral stimulation.

He may need to put some cushions under his bottom in the Little Dipper to boost himself so he can effectively permeate you it.

Tips

- If you want a triceps workout during sex, after that this is an ideal placement for

- The Little Dipper is likewise great for anal sex.

- Grinding on your man is far more fun and method much less exhausting than elevating on your own up and down on him.

Comments
Even though the Little Dipper is a uniqueness setting that looks a little ridiculous, I still believe that you ought to try it out with your male simply to keep points fascinating in the room. At least it will give both of you a few laughs 4k.

4k. Octopus Sex Position

The Octopus sex placement is something you have possibly never ever heard about. This is a good thing as it's something entirely new and also various for you and also your man to attempt.

In the Octopus placement, you can either muffle the bed (as in the picture over) or you can remain on his lap.

To perform it, initially get your man to sit down on the flooring and lean backwards somewhat, using his hands placed behind his back to sustain himself. If he spreads his legs, he will find it easier to balance. He then needs to flex his legs somewhat. You after that require to stand over him (feet either side of his waist) and gradually lower on your own (squat) onto his dick. When he is inside you, rest on his lap as well as slowly start to lean backwards. Put your hands behind your back on the ground for assistance. Once you are leaning in reverse, you after that need to lift your right leg and also remainder it on your male's left shoulder. Then lift your left leg as well as rest it on his right shoulder.

Girl roles

You may find that it gets tiring quite quickly as it's not the easiest thing to hold your body like this when you are in the octopus position. You can press on your own onto his penis during sex, yet this will just tire you out quicker. It's much better to just let him do all the thrusting.

By leaning in closer to your man's body or leaning backwards and away from his body, you can transform the angle he penetrates you at. If you do lean in, then cover your arms around the back of his neck to hold yourself in position. If you discover that you cannot perform the Octopus for a continual time period without your arms feeling like jelly, then attempt doing it close to a sofa to ensure that your back is leaning on the sofa as well as taking the majority of your weight.

Man roles

Your male is going to be doing a lot of embedding the Octopus position. So it's a good suggestion for him to see to it that both his hands and also feet can't conveniently slip. He can propelled backwards and forwards utilizing his hips while maintaining the remainder of his body in position. He can additionally shake his body to and fro using his legs and arms.

Your man might additionally discover this position to be truly exhausting. He should also consider leaning his back up against a couch or bed to take some of the weight off his arms if he does.

Tips

If both you as well as your male are not really in shape, after that you will both get tired of the Octopus very rapidly. I have actually heard from greater than one pupil that their arms seemed like jelly after less than a min of the Octopus. So if you aren't strong sufficient to perform it as described here, after that organize a bed or couch for you and your man to lean on, to take the weight off your arms.

You could locate that when executing the Octopus, your man will not have the ability to fuck you with wonderful long thrusts.

The best part of executing the Octopus with your man is that it's highly unlikely that he's ever before experienced it previously. So despite the fact that it's not the best sex position ever before, it's still something that will keep points interesting in the bedroom.

Comments

I directly do not take pleasure in the Octopus that a lot. It's also exhausting and also I find it simply doesn't do that much for me. However, prior to you determine against the Octopus lovemaking setting on your own, try it as well as see if it's something you like.

4l. Pearly Gates Sex Position

The Pearly Gates sex setting is not a crazy placement that calls for lots of flexibility or strength, but a lot of people have still never ever tried it.

Both you as well as your man will be encountering in the same direction. Your male will certainly be resting on his back on the bed with his knees bent and feet planted on the bed. You will be resting on top of him, also on your back with your head above his and sideways while your guy penetrates you. You will look like you're

spooning while facing the ceiling. To remain balanced while on top of your male, you require to spread out your legs and also flex them to make sure that you can keep your feet on the bed.

The Pearly Gates position is fantastic if you like the sensation of being revealed during sex.

You might also intend to spread your arms out too to remain balanced. Your man can after that wrap his arms around your waist or chest or under your arms, getting your shoulders.

Girl roles

When you initially try the Pearly Gates position, you are going to find it unpleasant to keep your balance, yet after a little, you will certainly get made use of to it. When you discover that you are no longer fretting about maintaining your balance, you'll find that you'll have the ability to thrust back onto your guy's penis as he is propelling right into you. You may even find that you can stabilize with simply one hand while utilizing your free hand to give some 'digital' stimulation to your clit.

Man roles

Your male has 2 jobs when in the Pearly Gates setting:

1) His first is assisting to keep you balanced by placing his arms around you. The tighter he holds you, the less that you'll need to do to maintain yourself balanced.

2) His second job is propelling into you from below. By flexing his knees as well as maintaining his feet on the bed, he can obtain a fair bit of leverage to do all the penetration so you can simply relax as well as enjoy it.

Tips

- There are a great deal of variations of the Pearly Gates that you can perform: You can put your arms behind you on your man's upper body or on the bed to make sure that you can increase yourself upwards. You can likewise bring your knees close to breast for a slightly different angle of access

When your man has his arms around you and is grabbing your shoulders, - Many appreciate the subjected sensation you experience.

- Your guy can reach downwards with one hand to start massaging your clitoris.

Remarks

The Pearly Gates position will certainly not be the initial position that enters your mind when you are having sex with your individual, however you must definitely try it (or it's variants) if you want find out new methods of making love as well as intend to keep things intriguing in the bed room.

4m. Piledriver Sex Position

The piledriver sex position is fairly an unique setting that requires a lot of adaptability. It can be very unpleasant to get into this placement with your guy. As well as soon as you are in it, it can actually be quite uncomfortable for both you and your male. One of the very best aspects of the piledriver position is that both anal and also vaginal sex are possible.

As you can see aware this is definitely a 'man-on-top' sex setting!

To carry out the pile vehicle driver love making position you require to first lay on your back. Following you require to raise your legs in the air. Your companion then needs to order the rear of your ankles as well as slowly push them towards your head. This will create your reduced back to begin lifting up off the bed. Ideally (if it's comfortable) your guy will certainly keep pushing your ankles towards your head until every one of your back is off the ground as well as the only point that's left on the ground is your shoulders as well as the back of your head.

This will certainly leave you very exposed (which is a genuine turn on for several). The man requires to maintain least one hand on your ankle joints so that he can hold you in place. To enter you, he will certainly need to point his penis downwards which can cause significant strain on his suspensory tendons.

Girl roles

You don't need to do anything at all other than to hold on your own constant when you are in the piledriver position. You can do this by putting your arms on the ground or by getting your male's ankle joints. When you remain in the piledriver placement, you will locate that it's extremely easy to masturbate which can make sex a lot even more enjoyable than typical.

Guy roles

Your guy needs to do the majority of the job. He requires to keep you stable while permeating you at the same time. After that he can use one of his hands to scrub your clit, if you are having vaginal sex. Or if you are having rectal sex, he can finger your vaginal canal while penetrating you.

If you like your male taking on a dominant role throughout sex, then you will certainly enjoy the Piledriver.

Leading Tip

A a lot easier means to enter this placement is to sit down on a couch the opposite way to how you generally would. This suggests that your back and also waistline is supported by the backrest while your shoulders and also head are where your bottom generally is. This will be much more comfy for you.

Tips
- Both of you require to be quite versatile.
- You should not execute it whatsoever if you have a weak or poor back.
- A small number of individuals (both girls and people) have said that they haven't got much from this setting.
- If you like feeling like your male is in complete control and also having him in a controlling setting, after that you will delight in the piledriver.
- The piledriver is wonderful if you like having anal sex while likewise having your vaginal canal promoted (fingers/vibrator/dildo).

4n. Piston Sex Position

The Piston sex position can be an incredibly fun and pleasing sex placement for both you and your man. It can obtain fairly exhausting really rapidly, which often makes it seem much more like Sexercise than sex. You can possibly presume that the name Piston originates from the reality that your male will certainly look a little bit like a piston in an engine, moving up as well as down when doing it.

The Piston setting is extremely comparable
in numerous means to the Pump position.

To execute the Piston, your male will be standing up directly. You will certainly be facing him as well as he will have raised you up off the ground as well as be holding you airborne, by putting his arms under your butt/thighs. Each leg will normally be on either side of your male. Your guy needs to perform the Piston with his back dealing with either a bed or a couch so that you can put you legs on the sofa/bed to help take a little of your weight. The most effective method to enter into the Piston placement is to begin with your guy sitting on the side of the bed with you straddling him so that it's very easy for him to get into the standing position.

Lady roles
Before you even attempt the Piston with your man, the first thing you require to do is judge whether you assume your man is strong enough to hold you. Fail to remember regarding the Piston and also assume concerning one more setting like the Mongolian Smurf or the Corner Cowgirl sex positions if you have any type of questions concerning his toughness.

As soon as you are positive that he is strong enough then it's time to do it. I advise that you start off straddling your guy while he's seated as well as after that having him stand up while holding you, but you can try it from a standing start. When your man is standing with his back near the sofa/bed, you can utilize your feet on the sofa/bed to give you utilize to help you move yourself up and down. You can likewise place your arms around his neck to hold on your own near him.

Male roles
Your man needs to ensure that he is safety of his back in the Piston setting. So if he doesn't feel like he is solid enough, then he should avoid the Piston entirely. If is solid sufficient, after that he should absolutely try it out. Just ensure that he maintains his back straight throughout.

All your guy requires to do in the Piston setting is just lower himself as well as raise himself somewhat utilizing his legs. He does also have the alternative of using his aware of embeded and also out also.

Tips

It can obtain tiring for your guy very rapidly.

Your male needs to be mindful when holding you by the butt/thighs so that he does not harm your skin by inadvertently stretching it with his hands by pulling on it too hard.

Comments

I find that the Piston is fantastic for when I want an adjustment and also to spice up sex.

However it's virtually excessive job to be fun a great deal of the moment.

4o. Scissors Sex Position

The Scissors is an extremely unique looking however fairly simple to perform sex position. This is one sex position that you may find tough to envision without a photo to explain it.

It might look challenging, yet the Scissors setting is rather easy.

To execute the Scissors sex setting with your male, start by lying on your side so that one leg is on the bed and also your other leg is right in addition to it. Following increase your leg as well as flex it to make sure that your guy has very easy access to your vaginal area. Your man is additionally mosting likely to be resting on his side. He will certainly be existing so that his head is close to your feet. He currently needs to slip his reduced leg underneath your lower leg right by your crotch.

Next off he will certainly put his upper leg over your lower leg and move his crotch in the direction of you until he can permeate you. Your lower leg will be between his legs. You will be pushing your side, facing far from your guy as well as he will certainly be dealing with towards your back. After he enters you, he simply needs to begin thrusting.

Girl roles

You first require to obtain comfortable when you are in the Scissors placement with your man. As you will certainly be pushing your man's thigh it can really feel a little awkward.

As soon as you are set up ready with your man, then all you require to do is 'go with the flow' of your male. To put it simply, gently returned onto your man as he is propelling into you. You'll locate that you are utilizing your whole body to returned right into your man, both your legs and also arms. You can grab hold of your male's leg(s) to give on your own some leverage to thrust back onto him.

Male roles

Your male additionally requires to make certain that he fits in the Scissors position. You will certainly be relaxing component of your weight on his leg! Once he is comfortable, after that he can simply concentrate on embedding and out as you thrust back onto him.

He'll be able to conveniently clinch your leading leg to pull himself in towards you as he is penetrating you.

When you perform the Scissors placement in front of a wall surface, you can push back against it with your hands for stronger propelling.

Tips

You might locate that you need to fiddle/fool about in the Scissors placement for a bit up until you discover an angle that you both delight in.

You can use your hand to offer yourself with some clitoral stimulation while performing the Scissors. Executing the Scissors setting on a solitary bed is difficult. You require room!

Comments

I like the Scissors position, specifically as an adjustment from normal sex

4p. Sockets Sex Position

The Sockets sex placement looks really comparable to the Scissor sex setting.
The reason is merely because it's a variation of the Scissors.
To execute the Sockets with your man, begin by lying on your back on the bed with your legs open and also expanded. After that flex your knees as well as plant your feet on the bed. This will permit you to raise you waistline as well as your lower withdraw the bed. Next, your guy is mosting likely to rest on his side at the opposite end of the bed, with his penis closest to your and his head furthest away. He then moves down in the direction of you to ensure that he can enter you.

As you can see aware above, the Sockets position is really similar to the Scissors setting.
He is going to slide his best leg under your left leg as well as put his left leg over your left leg if he is existing on his right-hand side. To enter you, he will certainly need to press his penis downwards which can cause a bit of stress and also pain if his penis is not that adaptable.

Woman roles
You will be a setting that you might have never ever attempted previously, yet after a few mins you need to obtain utilized to it. You are simply going to thrust forwards as well as in reverse onto your male in a kind of rocking motion utilizing your legs. You might discover that it tires you out really swiftly if you are not made use of to maintaining on your own raised off the bed like this.
You'll additionally need to spread out your arms a great little bit to aid you balance. Or you can try grabbing hold of one of his legs to assist pull yourself in towards him. Unwind and try relaxing an excellent component of your weight on his lower leg and grinding on him instead if you begin to get tired of thrusting against your guy.

Man roles
Your male will certainly remain in a bit of an awkward situation. As he gets on his side, he will not really have the ability to thrust in and also out. Rather, he should clinch your leg that's in front of him as well as delicately draw you in towards him as you are thrusting. He can hold onto your leg rather tightly to raise the rubbing if you are both grinding versus each other.

Entering the Sockets setting is not as easy as something like Doggy Style or Missionary.

Tips
The Sockets can be fairly an awkward setting to perform with your male as it quite unlike anything besides the Scissors.

If you locate it tedious maintaining your midsection held upwards, after that try putting a cushion under you back to offer you some assistance.

This is not an actually intimate position. It's also diffifult to make eye call during it.

Comments

The Sockets setting definitely looks unique, but the only tough feature of preforming it is making certain that your male has sufficient flexibility in his penis to draw it totally downwards. Other than that, it's actually straightforward.

4q. Carry & stand Sex Position

The Stand & Carry position is unlike pretty much every other sex position.
You don't need a couch or a bed to perform it.

Rather your male is mosting likely to be standing up for it and he will certainly be holding you off the ground. Lifting you up is the hardest part of the Stand & Carry. It's easiest is if you start of in a position like the Butterfly, with you resting on your back on a bed or a table, while your guy is standing.

Carrying out the Stand & Carry requires a good little toughness from both of you.

Your man can then lean over you and you can place your arms around the back of his neck and also wrap your legs around his waist. Your guy can put his arms around your waist or butt before standing up right while holding you.

You can both start off standing as well as encountering each other like in the Slow Dance setting. While inside you, your man can place his hands around your butt/waist and also pick you up. When your guy chooses you up you can then cover your legs around him.

Woman roles

When your male is holding you airborne, you need to carry some of your weight utilizing your arms around the back of his neck. Your legs twisted around his midsection can likewise bring several of your weight.

Despite the fact that your guy will certainly be doing a great deal of the thrusting, you can still draw on your own up and down on him. You can pull yourself up with your arms and you can squeeze your legs versus his waist to grasp it to ensure that you can relocate yourself upwards. When in the Stand & Carry setting, you can lean backwards a fair bit or hold yourself near to your male to alter the angle he enters you at.

Man roles

Your man has 2 work in the Stand & Carry setting. The initial is holding on to you and also supporting the majority of your weight. The 2nd is propelling right into you. He will be keeping you by wrapping his hands around your midsection. He can thrust right into you by flexing and also straightening his legs. Or he can use his hips while maintaining his legs relatively right.

Some pairs prefer executing the Stand & Carry setting against a wall.
Why not attempt both as well as see what you favor?

Tips

- The Stand & Carry is tiring: Performing it for more than 2-3 minutes is exhausting for both of you.

- Try performing the Carry & stand up against a wall, to ensure that your back is up against it. This will certainly aid take a few of your weight meaning you and also your guy can last much longer in it. He will likewise have the ability to fuck you with even more force when you protest a wall surface.

The Stand & Carry is not that tough to do. The only thing that it requires is that both of you have a significant amount of strength. If your man has a bad back, then I very suggest that he prevents the Stand & Carry as it will put a lot of stress on it.

4r. Swiss Miss Sex Position

The Swiss Miss Sex placement is absolutely one that falls under the classification of Exercise with your male. This is since you will certainly be utilizing your core muscular tissues to keep on your own stabilized on a Swiss physical fitness sphere (sometimes called a medicine ball, fitness round or health club ball. It's a big rubber inflatable sphere).

As you can see, the Swiss Miss placement is like a combination between Doggy Style as well as the Jockey positions.

To establish it up, you are first mosting likely to require a Swiss sphere. You require to lie on top of it with your belly, balancing with your hands in front of you. You can also put your feet on the ground behind you to help keep yourself balanced if it's small enough. If not, then simply use your hands and also keep your legs in the air. Your guy will certainly after that enter you from behind much like he would certainly in the Life Raft or Superwoman placements. He can hold on to your legs or waistline

Girl roles

When in the Swiss Miss setting, you need to focus the majority of your energy on keeping your equilibrium. This will be simpler if the Swiss round is a little one. You can also make it easier by jamming the Swiss ball into position (against a bed, sofa, etc.) before you start having sex in the Swiss Miss position.

You can push back onto your man by putting your hands on the wall if you are close to a wall when having sex in the Swiss Miss position.

If you are having a great deal of problem maintaining your equilibrium on your hands, curtail until you are balancing the majority of your weight on your feet. You'll discover this to be a great deal simpler.

Male roles

Although sex in the Swiss Miss position is a lot easier for your guy than you, he ought to first concentrate on making sure that you can balance on the Swiss ball properly. If you are having problem, then he requires to put his hands on your midsection to keep you stable.

When you are sure that you are remaining rather constant, he after that just needs to begin thrusting. That's it! He does need to be careful not to thrust too tough though, otherwise he may put a lot of stress on your hands and arms.

Covering your legs around your male is simply among the many various variations of the Swiss Miss you can do.

Tips

- It can obtain fairly strenuous on your arms extremely rapidly. If you discover your arms tiring, after that curtail to make sure that you stabilizing the majority of your weight on your feet rather.

- Try placing both of your legs with each other rather than apart for a somewhat various sensation.

- Don't fail to remember that anal sex is just as very easy as vaginal sex in the Swiss Miss setting.

4s. Tango Sex Position

The Tango sex setting gets it's name from the dance because of the fact that you need to be quite adaptable as well as contend the very least a little stamina to do it.

Your man can assist to sustain your back utilizing his hands in the Tango placement.

When doing the Tango, you will certainly remain in a placement similar to the Acrobat, other than that you will be resting on the bed as opposed to your male. To enter into the Tango position, you require to lie down on the bed on your back. Before you do, start on your knees, then slowly lie backwards, until your back is on the bed while your knees are too. See to it that your legs are fairly open, so that your male can easily penetrate you.

If you are not that adaptable, then put some cushions under your back for assistance.

Your man will after that be on his knees as well as will certainly permeate you equally as he would certainly in the Launch Pad position.

Lady roles

You will locate that you are in a really stable setting when carrying out the Tango with your man. So don't stress too much regarding pressing yourself back onto him when executing the Tango. Rather you ought to spend most of your time attempting to stay comfy. You will find that it can get uncomfortable quite quickly if you aren't that flexible and haven't performed either the Tango or Acrobat before.

You can likewise attempt the Tango while you have your legs held together. It will certainly likewise really feel a whole lot tighter for your guy.

Male roles

Your male's very first top priority is making certain that you are comfortable prior to he starts to permeate you.

There is no point in executing any type of sex setting if it triggers you pain!

As soon as you fit, then it's time for your man to start penetrating you. He ought to not put any of his weight on your when penetrating you, however should support everything via his hands and also knees. He conveniently change the angle of infiltration by leaning right over you, bring his weight through his hands on the bed or by leaning right back and holding your midsection with his hands.

Tips

Because your hips are raised right off the bed), - This position allows for a much different angle of angle of entry by your man (.

- If you are a dancer/gymnast/already adaptable, then you will certainly discover the Tango a lot, whole lot much easier.

- Do not try the Tango if you have poor knees!

- Some really appreciate the Tango due to the fact that their hips are elevated permitting a various angle of entrance, while others reported that it wasn't that great.

Comments

The Tango is a sex placement that few individuals have actually experimented with. Because of this, it may look like a 'rarer', extra exotic sex setting. Don't let this fool you: just because a sex position is 'rarer'/ exotic/' out there' does not necessarily mean that it's better or more fun or provides greater orgasms. Nonetheless, keeping that being said, the Tango is still fantastic to check out if you are searching for something brand-new.

4t. Wheel Barrow Sex Position

The Wheel Barrow sex position is extra a test of strength than a fun and enjoyable sex position for you and also your guy. Yet it can be fun to attempt once or twice if you find that things starting to obtain stale in the bedroom.

As you can see aware above, doing the Wheel Barrow is really tough. For many it really feels more like Sexercise.

To execute the Wheel Barrow, think back to when you were in school and also had 'wheel barrow' races. You would be facing towards the ground, resting a huge part of you weight on your hands with your arms prolonged. Your male would certainly after that be standing in between your legs and also holding them while you stroll onward. The Wheel Barrow sex setting is almost the same to this. You require to do every little thing the same as you typically would, except your guy will a lot better to you this time to make sure that he can permeate you.

Lady roles

You will discover that your arms and also hands get worn out incredibly swiftly when you are in the Wheel Barrow placement. You may find that you are exhausted after less than a min of performing it. As your guy is thrusting in and also out, you simply require to try and also maintain your equilibrium. That's basically it.

To aid carry some of your weight, you can try pressing your legs around your male.

Male roles

If you plan on doing the Wheel Barrow position with your guy, then see to it that he knows just how tiring it can be for you. In this manner, he will certainly recognize to help bring some of your weight throughout it. He should lean onward somewhat and put his hands under your waistline to assist hold you up. He can place a cushion under your waist as well as hold either side of it. You'll locate this much a lot more comfy and less painful than having your man order you.

Your male will make it harder for you to balance if he begins thrusting forwards as well as backwards, pressing you forwards and backwards as he does. It's better if he can do an extra 'backwards and forwards' motion as it will permit you to remain steady more easily.

Tips

- Anal sex can be done fairly conveniently in the Wheel Barrow placement.

If you are interested in Sexercise as it is really hard on your shoulders and also arms, - The Wheel Barrow is ideal.

Chapter 5. Lying On Your Side Sex Positions

Pushing your side can make for some actually slow & sensuous sex for both you and your guy. If you are exhausted or would favor your man to do the mass of the job throughout sex, after that you should attempt a few of the se resting on your side placements. A lot of the se placements additionally include Spooning or a variant of Spooning, which is virtually the most intimate lovemaking setting you can do with your man.: Intersection Position, Irish Spooning, Position, Leg Glider Position, Mongolian Smurf Position, Poles Apart Position, Screw Position, Side Entry Missionary Position, Sofa Spooning Position, Spooning Position, Sporking Position, Twister Position

5a. Intersection Sex Position

The intersection is a position that very few people have attempted prior to. You will certainly be developing a cross with your bodies when doing it, similar to exactly how your bodies will form a cross in the Cross setting.

To get involved in the Intersection placement, you and also your guy require to both lie on your sides. You need to lie with your head at the top of the bed as well as feet at the end of the bed. Your man will certainly be existing throughout the bed, with his feet on one side and his directly the opposite side of the bed. You require to open your legs to make sure that your male can relax on top of your lower leg and after that penetrate you. Then you can rest your top leg in addition to his legs.

Relocating from the Spooning position to the Intersection position is truly simple.

Girl roles
This position can be a little unpleasant at first, so before your male starts propelling, make certain that you are both comfy. Your man is going to be in between your legs and also relaxing several of his weight on your lower leg. Because of this he can quickly remove your circulation, so make sure to inform him if it begins to obtain uneasy or if you start getting pins and needles. As a result of the placement you're in, you will locate it relatively hard to do much returning onto your man. Thankfully however, you can masturbate in this setting and even finger yourself if you are having rectal sex.

Guy roles!
Your male requires to be cautious in the Intersection position. If he is a lot larger than you, after that he needs to ensure he does not put all his weight on your leg, possibly removing your blood circulation. To aid keep his legs off you, he needs to place some cushions under his legs.

All your male needs to do is to thrust in as well as out of you. The challenging component for him is getting himself into a placement that fits for him as well as you which likewise enables him to propelled into you easily. He'll discover that spreading his legs will assist him to obtain enough take advantage of to thrust into you.

Tips
If your guy is particularly hefty, then prevent this setting. It will certainly harm greater than it feels fun for you.

If you desire, you can do a minor variant of the Intersection setting with your man. Rather than allowing your male rest his legs in addition to yours, bring your legs close to your belly to make sure that they run out the method. This will certainly make the Intersection really feel more like a quasi-spooning setting.

5b. Irish Spooning Sex Position

The Irish Spooning placement is a truly good and also relaxed sex setting for both you as well as your male. As this is a spooning setting, you'll find that it's additionally really intimate for both of you.

To enter into the Irish Spooning position, you require to get into the recovery setting. This suggests that you need to rest on your side. You lower leg will be fairly right, while you need to elevate your knee of your top leg in the direction of your chest and after that flex it and also relax it on the bed. Rest the arm joint from your leading arm on the bed in front of your as well as rest your lower arm above it.

Your male then enters you from behind on his side. He can enter you like he typically would when Spooning you or he can bend his leading leg like yours as well as rest it behind your top leg and relax his lower leg behind your bottom leg. He then needs to wrap his leading arm around you and afterwards figure out a method of placing his bottom arm in such a way that is comfortable for both of you.

A fantastic method to position his bottom arm is to just leave it relaxing right over his head to ensure that he looks virtually like Superman.

Woman roles

Spooning is a truly intimate and sensuous placement that you don't have to be that energetic for. You actually don't need to do anything if just want to loosen up, yet you can start massaging your clitoris to aid you orgasm. Or if you are having rectal sex, then you can likewise finger yourself.

Your man will certainly like it if you reach back as well as put your arm on his back/butt and rub it.

Man roles

Your male will certainly be slowly embedding as well as out of you. Irish Spooning is not about hardcore, enthusiastic sex. It's loving as well as around sluggish sex. He just requires to keep up a wonderful regular rhythm while holding you snugly. Additionally he can slowly grind up against you.

To contribute to the intimacy, he can delicately kiss you on your neck, back as well as ears.

Tips

- The Irish Spooning position allows you to easily have rectal sex. If you do not specifically enjoy anal sex with your man, after that prevent it when Irish Spooning.

5c. Leg Glider Sex Position

The leg glider is an extremely unique sex placement that it rather hard to perform appropriately unless you have a bargain of versatility, although your guy does not need to be that versatile to do it.

To properly perform the Leg Glider you need to be fairly versatile!

To do the Leg Glider, you just need to rest on one side, let's state your left side. This suggests that your left leg, left side and left arm will certainly get on the bed. Your ideal leg will be hing on top of your left leg and your ideal arm will be hing on your body, although you can put your right-hand man on the bed to steady yourself if you want. You after that require to elevate your ideal leg in the direction of the ceiling while keeping your left leg on the bed. Your best leg ought to be aiming straight towards the ceiling if you are flexible enough.

Preferably your legs must be at 90 levels (the right leg aiming straight up to the ceiling as well as your left one lying on the bed directing in the direction of the wall.

Your male then starts on his knees and as well as remains upright. He will certainly be straddling your left leg. He will aid support your best leg on his chest/shoulder.

Lady roles

When you remain in the Leg Glider placement, your primary goal is to maintain stable as well as stay in placement without your legs cramping up. If you do feel your legs starting to cramp up, then tell your man promptly so that you can extend them as well as get rid of the ache.

You'll locate it far simpler to perform the Leg Glider if you flex both knees slightly. Certainly heating up ahead of time is an excellent concept too.

Man roles

When your guy is performing the Leg Glider, in the beginning he requires to be mindful to make certain that you fit and that he is not placing excessive stress on your leg. If he is well put up, he requires to be careful that he is not penetrating you as well deeply.

As soon as you get into a nice rhythm with your male in the Leg Glider, he can get the base of your best leg or hold onto your appropriate arm to ensure that he can pull you towards him and also penetrate you a lot more deeply. Your man can likewise lean backwards to transform the angle of entrance as well as forwards (simply make certain that he is really cautious when he is leaning forwards not to injure you). In addition to leaning up and down, he can transfer to one side or the various other until he finds the setting that you both appreciate many.

Tips

If you have a lot of versatility, after that your male can permeate you truly deeply, by pushing your leg that's pointing towards the ceiling further out of the way.

Stretching your legs ahead of time is an excellent suggestion as it will make this position a whole lot less complicated for you.

If you are not that flexible, however still want to perform the Leg Glider with your man, after that you can, by getting your man to lean backwards to make sure that you don't have to stretch you leg as much.

While your male has even more control in this position than you, you must see to it that he takes care not to hurt you.

Comments

I find the Leg Glider to be an excellent change from the regular sex positions like doggy style, the anvil and also missionary. My suggestions is to try it a minimum of when and afterwards make a decision later if you like it or otherwise.

5d. Mongolian Smurf Sex Position

The Mongolian Smurf sex placement is a really satisfying man on top placement, where you can loosen up as well as allow your guy do pretty much every one of the work.

To carry out the Mongolian Smurf, you'll need to lie on your side in the recovery setting similar to you would for the Irish Spooning position. Then you require to increase you top leg a little towards your upper body and place your top arm either ahead or behind you to stay in position. You can maintain your lower leg fairly straight and feel free to position your reduced arm nonetheless you such as. Your guy after that requires to straddle your straight leg while on his knees and also stay upright and begin propelling into you. You will not have the ability to do anything in this position so you can simply relax as well as rest.

In spite of the amusing name, performing the Mongolian Smurf is actually easy.

Woman roles
Like I just said, you don't require to do anything in the Mongolian Smurf position. You simply need to loosen up. If you want though, you can use among your hands to begin masturbating on your own as well as massaging your clitoris to help yourself orgasm. If you are having anal sex with your guy, then you can finger on your own as well.

Guy roles
Your man will be doing nearly all the work. He can relax his hands on the bed to make it easier to propelled right into you or he can put his hands on your waist/leg. If you desire him to thrust deeper into you, then your man can grab your arm and pull you in the direction of him with each drive.

But also for a lot of pairs, the Mongolian Smurf is not all about penetrating you quickly as well as hard, it's regarding slower, more intimate as well as mild sex. This suggests that your male may intend to slow down things down a bit and also grind on you rather than thrusting in as well as out.

Tips
When you are tired and you want your male to do all the work, - The Mongolian Smurf is wonderful for.

- The Mongolian Smurf is more of a sensuous sex setting than an insane, 'wild' sex setting. If he wants, your man can permeate you more intensely if he desires.

- Anal sex is fairly simple in the Mongolian Smurf setting, however it doesn't make for a sensuous, intimate time with your male.

- To aid your guy penetrate you much deeper, you can grab your top leg with you arms(s) as well as pull it closer to your chest.

Remarks
It's really easy to change from Irish Spooning to the Mongolian Smurf immediately.

5e. Poles Apart Sex Position

The Poles Apart sex position is practically definitely not one that you have actually attempted prior to with your partner. It's even a little difficult to envision. However some pairs definitely love it as offers a great deal of G-Spot excitement without really deep infiltration.

To get into the Poles Apart position, you both need to lie on your sides, dealing with in the same direction. This appears just the Spoons placement, however it's not. As opposed to lying with your head in front of your male's head, you require to alter your setting so that your head is currently in front of his feet and also your feet remain in front of his head. Simply put you need to be existing head to toe with your guy. Your male after that enters you from behind either vaginally or anally.

The Poles Apart setting is a good variant on Spooning.

Lady roles
When you first get involved in the Poles Apart placement, you may discover it practically a little bit disorientating to be existing head to toe with your man. However in many means the Poles Apart setting is just like Spooning, just take things sluggish as well as steady. You'll discover that maintaining your guy from 'bulging' can be a little difficult when you are both lying directly, so if you like, do not hesitate to flex your body a little bit to keep him inside you.

All you need to do is simply push back versus your male as he is propelling right into you. If you are having anal sex, you will certainly additionally be able to massage yourself or also finger yourself.

Male roles
When in the Poles Apart sex placement, your guy is going to be doing the same actions as he would certainly be doing if your were both Spooning. This implies that he will be carefully thrusting into you. To give himself some grasp and utilize, he will certainly discover that keeping your legs will certainly aid him to permeate your deeper.

If you appreciate your guy having fun with your feet, then the Poles Apart placement is excellent for this. They will typically be right in front of his face or just listed below it so that he can use his hands as well as mouth to kiss as well as massage them.

Your man can grab your legs in the Poles Apart position as well as you can get to behind and order his butt to draw yourself in with each thrust.

Tips
The Poles Apart position is perfect for both genital and also anal intercourse

Even though your bodies will be in close get in touch with, it can seem like it's not that intimate for some as your mouths and eyes are so far away from each other.

The Poles Apart setting is really relatively easy to do (you just require a little bit of penile versatility). This makes is a fantastic placement for spicing things up in the bed room.

5f. Screw Sex Position

The Screw sex placement is truly very easy to perform even though a great deal of couples have not tried it previously. It's a terrific position to try out with your male, especially if you are just beginning to try out brand-new sex positions. In many means, it's rather comparable to the Drill or Anvil sex position.

You need to start off by resting on your side to do the Screw. After that once you are, draw your knees right up to your breast so your groin area is truly subjected. Your guy will certainly then get on his knees facing towards you and will begin penetrating you. To get down you your level, you man will require to spread his knees quite far apart. If he can not, after that attempt putting a cushion under you aware of elevate on your own up or your male can stoop on the floor as opposed to the bed to obtain the angles right.

The screw is extremely similar sideways Entry Missionary position. When doing the Screw, you will certainly have both your legs together on one side of your man.

Woman roles
As you are executing the Screw with your male, you'll find that you are rather stable and can't actually do a great deal. You won't actually be able to returned onto your male. The most you can do is just hold yourself in position and also grind on your male. You can carry out a minor variation on the Screw by putting your legs around the rear of your guy's legs and also pulling him in closer to you with each thrust.

Man roles
Your guy has a very simple job in the Screw position. It actually is simply a situation of thrusting in as well as out for him. If he likes, he can hold onto you by grabbing your legs or also ordering your arm. He can begin grinding on you rather if he desire's to take a break from thrusting.

As your guy gets on top of you, he will be a more dominant position and also can quickly lean over as well as start rubbing your breasts with his hands. He might discover leaning right over to kiss you a little harder though.

The Screw is wonderful for both genital and rectal sex.

Tips
Even though you need to bring your knees to your upper body to perform the Screw, you do not have to draw them right up, implying you don't require a substantial quantity adaptability in all to execute it, making it excellent for nearly everyone.

The Screw is equally helpful for those that like rectal sex as it is for those who like regular vaginal sex.

The Screw is not the most intimate sex placement.

Comments

I such as the Screw a lot. I would recommend it to any individual who is first starting with attempting to improve their sex life. I would certainly likewise recommend it to any person who intends to add one more easy-to-do position to their collection.

5g. Side Entry Missionary Sex Position

It's called the Side Entry Missionary setting, it's actually does not look a lot like the missionary setting at all.

You will certainly be resting on your side on the bed with your legs with each other and also curved. Most women are versatile enough in this placement to turn and encounter their man to raise the affection. Meanwhile your male will certainly be on his knees and will certainly enter you from behind. So your man will certainly remain in the very same setting he normally is when performing the missionary position, while you will remain in a new setting.

Relocating from Spooning sideways Entry Missionary placement is really easy.

Lady roles
You will certainly discover it hard to move with your male on top of you when you are in the Side Entry Missionary placement. So it will certainly be hard to thrust back onto him. You will certainly have both hands complimentary to place about your man's neck and also back. You can also pull him in the direction of you to kiss him as well. By raising your legs closer to your tummy or straightening them, you can manage exactly how deeply he penetrates you.

Guy roles
When your man is in the Side Entry Missionary setting, he will be doing a lot of the work. He can simply state on his knees as well as hands as well as maintain embedding and also out. But this will obtain a little boring after a while. He requires to move around somewhat till he finds the appropriate area. When I say walk around, I suggest relocate a little to the left or a little to the right (i.e. closer to your back or closer to your belly up until he is striking one of the most pleasant areas for you.

He can lean right over you and begin kissing you if he wants to make it more intimate. He can order your shoulders if he wants to permeate you with more intensity while leaning over you. Or if he is upright on his knees, he can put his hands on your top hip and also draw you in with each stroke.

You can change how deep you take your guy by just how you place your legs.

Tips
It' suite easy to transfer from regular Missionary to Side Entry Missionary with no loss of intimacy.

You might not get that much from it up until your male tries out a great deal of various angles, by moving somewhat to the left or to the right when entering you.

This setting is great for rectal sex also.

If you are not that adaptable, it's great to rest on your shoulder while in this position. Or you can even think the foetal position.

Comments

This position is great for couples who obtain burnt out of routine missionary. I highly encourage that you experiment with resting on both sides when doing the Side Entry Missionary

5h. Couch Spooning Sex Position

The Sofa Spooning sex position is a small variant of the normal Spooning position. To execute it with your individual, you will need a full size, comfortable couch. Couch Spooning creates wonderful sex when you are both alone on a Saturday early morning and want to enjoy some TV.

Sofa Spooning is an actually fantastic method to snuggle up to your male while seeing TELEVISION.

To establish on your own up in the Sofa Spooning setting, your guy initially needs to rest on the sofa with his back firmly versus the backrest part of the couch. Then you need to rest in front of him while encountering in the same direction. Your man then enters you from behind and starts to gradually thrust into you while covering his arms around you.

Woman roles

The Sofa Spooning placement is great if you such as to just kick back and allow your man take control. There isn't much you need to do, besides just lie there. If you like, then you can gradually push on your own back onto your guy with each stroke.

When Sofa Spooning with your guy, you are likewise in an ideal position to gradually start masturbating on your own. All you need to do is just decrease your hand and begin massaging the outside of your vaginal area.

Guy roles

Your male's major work in the Sofa Spooning setting is entering into a wonderful rhythm while thrusting into you. Spooning is not expected to be a 'hardcore', harsh sex setting. Rather it's a slow-moving and sensual setting that's actually intimate. If your man doesn't understand this, after that allow him understand.

He can likewise enhance the affection of Sofa Spooning by covering his arms around you and also holding you near him. He is likewise in the excellent placement to reduce his hand as well as begin rubbing the outside of your vaginal canal.

If he locates that his arm covered under you is starting to obtain numb or aching, after that he can attempt putting it over his head in a kind of 'Superman' pose.

Tips

Most notably, ensure that your couch suffices for both of you. In other words see to it that it's long sufficient, deep enough and that the armrests will not be in your method.

Try putting a towel or sheet underneath both of you by your crotch location to shield your couch from any kind of physical fluid you don't desire on it.

Sofa Spooning is ideal for rectal sex also.

Remarks

I am a massive fan of the Sofa Spooning sex setting. When you just desire to see some TV while having sex at the same time, it's excellent for some actually slow-moving and sensual sex with your companion or.

5i. Spooning Sex Position

Spooning is among the standards along with the Missionary, Cowgirl as well as Doggy Style sex positions. It's not a sex setting for rough or 'hardcore' sex. Instead it's even more for those that take pleasure in sluggish, intimate sex with their man as your bodies are in complete contact with each other.

Spooning is actually very easy. It's a whole lot like the Sofa Spooning setting except it's executed in bed. You and also your man both need to lie on your sides, facing in the same direction. Your man will be behind you and after that requires to enter you. When in the Spooning placement, you need to bring your leading leg ahead a little bit to make it simpler for your man to penetrate you. Once he has entered you, he can wrap his arms around you for closeness.

As you can see in the picture, Spooning makes for some sensual and actually intimate sex with your man.

Girl roles

When you are Spooning with your man, you can push back versus him with each thrust. You can likewise play around with your setting by flexing forwards a little or lifting your legs towards your stomach to change the angle that your male is entering you at.

Guy roles

Like I have claimed prior to, Spooning is really easy. Your guy does not need to be strong or flexible at all to Spoon with you. He simply requires to thrust in and also out of you while on his side. He might find it less complicated to propelled right into you if he leans over you somewhat.

Your man is likewise in the best placement to get to about and begin masturbating you, by scrubing around your clitoris and labia with his fingers. He can likewise grab the top side of your midsection to make sure that he can thrust right into with a little more force. If your man places his arms around you, after that his reduced arm may become numb or get pins and also needles if he keeps it there for also lengthy. To stop this from taking place, he can put it behind your back or stretch it out over him (which looks a little like Superman flying).

Tips

- Spooning is ideal if you have just woken up or if you are really exhausted as well as you do not intend to do too much throughout it.

If you want to feel really physically close to your companion during sex, - Spooning is best.

- You can perform anal sex while Spooning with your guy.

Remarks

Like almost everyone else, I am a substantial fan of Spooning. Particularly when it's with a person that you are actually close to if feels remarkable. If haven't currently, I highly advise you try it with your man.

5j. Sporking Sex Position

The Sporking sex placement is really simply a variation of the Spooning position with your man. It's really great for those of you who are a little bigger as well as locate regular Spooning to be challenging.

To get into the Sporking placement with your man, just rest on your side with your man likewise pushing his side right behind you. You after that need to lean forwards and bring your legs towards your upper body while still lying on your side. There is no demand to lean right over or bring your legs rather near to your upper body like in the photo. It's mainly simply to change the angle that your man is permeating you at. On the other hand you man will certainly stay in basically the same placement.

As you can see in the picture, Sporking is extremely comparable to Spooning.

Lady roles

You simply need to relocate around by leaning forwards or backwards and also bending your legs or by correcting them out when you are in the Sporking position. If you are having anal sex with your guy, you will also be in a placement to rub yourself to assist you climax and also even finger on your own.

You can put your top arm in reverse to draw your guy into you as he is propelling as well. Apart from that though, Sporking is a fairly passive placement for you. Your guy will be doing most of the job.

Man roles

Your man will be doing the very same things that he does when he is in the Spoons position with you. So he will certainly be resting on his side while carefully thrusting right into you. He can place his top arm around your shoulders and pull you in close to him or he can grab hold of your waistline to help drive right into you. If you are having rectal sex with him, then he can get to around as well as start to massage therapy your clit and also finger you.

If your back is close to him, then he can kiss it and also can kiss you on your neck as well as your cheeks if you turn around a little bit.

Sporking is terrific if you enjoy the intimacy of Spooning, but intend to alter the angle of entry.

Tips

Many find that Sporking is equally as good as Spooning. It's just as satisfying however there is additionally a great deal more variant to it.

You can try leaning over a little onto your belly while in the Sporking setting additionally, to ensure that it's kind of like a mix in between Sporking and also Doggy Style.

If you are in front of a wall when Sporking, after that you can put your distribute before you and also push back against your man for harder penetration.

Comments

I like Sporking just as high as I like Spooning. They are both very comparable as well as are both excellent for when you desire some slower, a lot more intimate sex.

5k. Whirlwind Sex Position

The Twister sex placement is one of the most unique. When you perform it, it looks actually 'out there'. Like I constantly claim, simply because a lovemaking setting is exotic, doesn't mean that it's far better. Additionally, simply to be clear, the Twister sex position has nothing to do with the game called Twister.

To execute the Twister sex setting with your guy, you initially need to relax on your side, claim your best side. Your man will certainly also be lying down on his right side, with his tummy facing your tummy, yet you will be lying head-to- toe with your man. This implies that your head needs to be close you his feet. Both of you require to flex your left knees as well as elevate them towards the ceiling. This will certainly develop a void in between his legs (and also your own).

You then require to lean ahead and press your body via this space so that your male's elevated left leg is currently above your waist, with you under it, however over his ideal leg. He will certainly also be sandwiched between your legs with your left leg over his midsection as well as right leg below. Your man must currently enter you and also begin propelling.

If you think this appears challenging, you're ideal it is! It takes some practice prior to you will get utilized to it.

Girl roles

When you initially try the Twister with your man, you'll discover that it takes a bit to obtain totally comfy with it. An essential thing to do is to hinge on your elbow joint as well as elevate your midsection off the bed. This will certainly stop you from placing all of your weight on his lower leg, which can possibly cut off his flow, making for some agonizing pins & needles!

You can also hold onto his butt and also pull yourself in every single time he drives.

Guy roles

Your guy will certainly be in much the same position as you. He needs to see to it that he's not accidentally relaxing his weight on your reduced leg, which will certainly remove your circulation. Before he starts strongly thrusting, he should make sure that both of you are completely comfy in the Twister and that he's not going to accidentally elope.

Tips

The finest aspect of the Twister is that it enables an angle of penetration that's quite different.

The Twister is an awkward placement to start with, so if neither of you are appreciating it that a lot, just attempt something else instead.

Remarks

When with your guy, my guidance on the Twister is to try it at the very least. If neither of you obtain much enjoyment out of it, the really fun point regarding it is that it's fantastic for spicing points up also.

Chapter 6. Resting on Your Back Sex Positions

There are lots of placements when lying on your back. This is wonderful for those that like their man ahead. These sex positions all include pushing your back. This consists of probably the most renowned of all sex positions, Missionary. If you prefer your guy to be in a much more dominant placement than you during sex, then you should attempt several of the positions: Anvil Position, Bent Spoon Position, Brute Position, Butterfly Position, Coital Alignment Technique, Cowboy Position, Criss-Cross Position, Cross Position, Deckchair Position,. Deep Impact Position, Down Stroke Position, Drill Position, Exposed Eagle Position, Hang Loose Position, Italian Hanger Position, Launch Pad Position, Missionary Position, Missionary 180 Sex Position, Pirates Bounty Position, Playing Of the Cello Position,. Angle Sex Position, Sandwich Position, Tug Of Love Position, Victory Position, Viennese Oyster Position, X Marks The Spot Position

6. a Anvil Sex Position

The anvil sex setting is a variation of the missionary placement. It's really simple to change to when you are currently having missionary sex with your man. The image listed below programs you specifically how to perform the anvil position with your

guy.

The Anvil is a really good variation on the Deckchair placement.

To make love in the anvil position, you just need to lay on your back, like you would when in the missionary placement. Just like when you remain in the missionary position, you need to spread your legs. Rather of relaxing them on your bed, you need to draw them shut to your breast. Your male after that positions himself over you. But instead of resting on his arm joints, he will certainly be hing on his hands. With the help of your guy, place your legs so that your calves/ankles are hing on his shoulders on either side of his neck.

Male roles

With your legs in this setting, your male will certainly currently be more conveniently able to rub his pubic bone over your clitoris to promote it. He can do this by carrying out a backward and forward motion where he is not actually moving in and out that much, but instead simply massaging over your clitoris as well as clitoral hood.

In this position, your guy can likewise penetrate you exceptionally deeply. If you like taking him deep, this is great. However if your male has a lengthy penis, then you'll discover that he will certainly strike the end of vagina where it accompanies the cervix which can cause significant pain. If he is triggering you any type of discomfort by permeating you too deeply, make sure to inform him instantly.

Lady roles

When you remain in the anvil placement, you might feel that your man is in control, however you'll discover that you can in fact push him off you utilizing your legs if you desire (unless obviously he is hefty as well as extremely huge!). This is fantastic as it implies that you can control how deep he penetrates you, implying that you'll almost always have the ability to locate a 'place' that really feels wonderful for you.

When you are in the anvil sex setting with your guy, you'll locate that he will not be as 'close' to you as your legs and in the method. Nonetheless, if you want to add affection to it you can carefully massage and damage his arms when they are either side of you.

Tips
- You need a bit of adaptability for this sex setting to be comfy for

- The more flexible and fit you are, the longer that you'll be able to hold this position before you obtain tired/sore/cramp.

If you are little or your guy has a long penis, after that it's rather most likely that he will permeate you also deeply when in this setting resulting in significant pain.

When you find 'the best place' it is incredibly pleasing.

Remarks

The wonderful aspect of the anvil setting is that it's actually straightforward placement to change to after doing missionary for a while. It additionally feels fairly various as it allows for much deeper penetration by the male. The anvil is additionally a great position for those who like their man in addition to them while still having a good quantity of control.

6b. Bent Spoon Sex Position

The Bent Spoon sex setting is kind of a combination between Spooning and also other placements. It's not the most preferred sex setting, however it can be fantastic if you are seeking to do something various and transform points up in the room with your man.

You'll find that it's a little hard to balance on your own at first in the Bent Spoon placement.

To perform it, your male requires to lie on his back. You then need to rest on top of him on your back to make sure that you are both encountering parallel. Permit your guy to enter you. Next, spread your arms outwards to keep on your own stable while obtaining your guy to spread his legs to maintain himself balanced. You need to bring your knees up in the direction of your chest and relax your feet on the tops of his knees for extra support when you are both constant.

Girl roles

When you are doing the Bent Spoon with your guy, you will be spending a lot of your time maintaining on your own steady with your arms and also keeping your legs close your upper body. The even more you draw your legs into your upper body, the shallower the infiltration will be. Trying out exactly how close your hold them up until your locate a place that offers you the very best experiences. If you can curve your back while performing the Bent Spoon, then your man will have the ability to much more deeply permeate you.

If you can maintain yourself steady with one hand, after that you can utilize your various other to rub your clitoris and also around your vaginal area.

Man roles

When executing the Bent Spoon, your guy must flex his knees and plant his feet on the bed to assist him to balance, but additionally to even more quickly thrust into you. Your male can additionally hold you in place by covering his arms around you, which leaves your arms complimentary to draw your legs near your belly as well as upper body. He is also in the ideal setting for massaging your breasts.

If he tries to take lengthy strokes, your man will certainly slide out extremely quickly. This suggests that he ought to try taking brief as well as quick strokes rather.

Tips

For some pairs, their is so little penetration that it's a virtually meaningless placement for both, either due to the fact that your guy will maintain slipping out, or you simply will not feel a lot from it.

Many of those who tried the Bent Spoon setting while having rectal sex favored it to vaginal sex.

Although you get on top of your guy in the Bent Spoon, he can still tackle a leading role by placing his hand on your neck or by ordering your hair and drawing it gently

If you are bigger than your man, he might discover it uneasy and fairly tough with your in addition to him.

Comments

I locate that the Bent Spoon position is fantastic for ladies that like a lot of G-Spot stimulation instead of extremely deep penetration

6c. Brute Sex Position

The Brute sex setting is a guy ahead position in which your man will certainly be quite leading however it's not specifically intimate. Somehow, the Brute is a little like the Amazon position but in reverse, with him on the top and also you on your back.

To get involved in this setting, you need to lie on your back as well as bring your knees to your stomach as well as chest. Your guy will certainly be standing with his back to you with his legs straddling your hips. He will certainly then squat downwards as well as slowly enter you. All he after that needs to do is gradually squat up and down.

As you can see aware, the Brute setting is very like the Amazon yet backwards.

When getting into this placement, you and your guy require to be really careful. He will certainly be pressing his penis really much downwards in order to permeate you, placing a great deal of pressure on his suspensory ligaments which can trigger him significant pain and also even injure him.

Lady roles

In the Brute setting, you do not have to do much. Initially your primary worry will be making sure that your male doesn't press too hard downward on your thighs with each thrust (it can be actually aching if your guy is rather big and also hefty). Apart from that, you just require to carefully push him back upwards using your upper legs. You can in fact put your feet under his underarms to assist push him up-wards if you want.

Male roles

Your man requires to be very cautious at first not to hurt himself in the Brute position. He will be pressing his penis very far downward just to enter you, so he ought to be gentle as well as very slow-moving with his initial few strokes.

An excellent way to take a few of the strain off his penis is for him to lean forwards.

The Brute placement doesn't allow your man to achieve deep infiltration, so he needs to focus on making small, short thrusts backwards and forwards, which can take a while to get made use of to at first. He might locate that as opposed to thrusting upwards and also downwards, it's simpler to remain relatively fixed as well as to just utilize his aware of grind on you.

Tips

- This is one of the least intimate/romantic positions out there. That's why it's called the Brute I mean.

- If your male takes pleasure in viewing porn throughout sex, then the Brute is an excellent placement for it. This is again another reason why this placement is not specifically intimate.

- Your guy needs to be actually careful not to thrust down as well hard, or else he can actually stretch and also hurt the muscles in your upper legs

6d. Butterfly Sex Position

The butterfly position is wonderful whether you remain in bed or on a table. The image listed below provides a terrific summary on how to execute the butterfly. There are a couple of really essential things to bear in mind though to ensure you get the most out of this setting.

Unless you have an extremely high bed, you'll require a table to carry out the Butterfly placement on.

Carrying out the butterfly is very simple for women. As I simply said, you can do it on a table or on a bed, it's truly approximately you. In the layout over, the man is standing, yet he can additionally be on his knees if you are using a bed.

You do not have to be that energetic when in the butterfly placement, while your male will need to do most of the work. All you need to do is to lie back while your man lifts your hips upwards. You can relax your thighs on his upper body as well as

place your reduced leg over his shoulder, just as in the picture. Conversely you can just place your legs either side of his midsection. My advice is to just do what you locate to be most comfy.

Man roles

I really believe that you will such as the butterfly for sex, especially if you are tired. This is since your male will have to do most of the work, while you get to lie back as well as enjoy it! In the layout above, the man has his hands under the women' hips and also is raising them up. This is great, but if he wishes to penetrate her more vigorously, he can hold her upper legs which will certainly make things a great deal less complicated for a more powerful penetration.

When he is standing as opposed to when he is stooping, he will additionally locate that he can relocate additionally forwards and also in reverse.

Girl roles

When you are in the butterfly, you merely need to rest on your back as well as either put your legs around your males' waist or rather enable them to hinge on his upper body and also over his shoulders.

While you can be really lazy as well as can let your guy do whatever, you might locate that you obtain more satisfaction by controlling exactly how high your hips are raised. When your legs are on his breast as well as over his shoulders, this is easiest. Due to the fact that your hips are increased, your male's penis will be in direct contact with the top wall surface of your vaginal area, enabling him to straight stimulate your G-Spot, which can bring about terrific climaxes. You can additionally utilize your belly (abdominals) to assist keep your legs increased, yet you'll find that they swiftly tire.

Tips

Using pillows or paddings under your hips/waist is a fantastic concept. It indicates that your man will not get too weary from holding your boosts and you won't obtain tired from attempting to keep them increased either.

If your male gets on his knees, it might be an excellent idea to place a pillow under them to make certain that they do not obtain hurt.

To get maximum pleasure from this position and make it less complicated for your male to hit your G Spot, make sure that your hip are somewhat more than his.

Keep adjusting how high you hold your hips up until you locate the right place. Believe me, it's worth it!

Remarks

If you see that your companion is burning out carrying out the butterfly, after that it might be an excellent concept to switch positions to something like the anvil or another thing or conversely get a cushion to put under your aware of give his arms a rest.

6e. Coital Alignment Technique Sex Position

If you like clitoral stimulation, the Coital Alignment Technique sex positions is terrific. To perform it with your guy, you require to push your back with your legs open while your guy is on top of you, much like in the routine missionary setting.

Yet instead of thrusting deeply in and out, your man requires to move his body forward over your body. This will certainly transform the angle that your man's penis enters you. It will currently be pointing downwards and also will certainly remain in greater contact with the lower wall of your vaginal area (the contrary side to your G-Spot). When you guy is this setting, his pubic bone (and sometimes the lower area of his penis) will extra quickly come into contact with your clitoris.

The Coital Alignment Technique resembles the Missionary setting, except that it's even more of a grinding activity instead of thrusting in & out like you do when doing Missionary.

Girl roles

When you are in the CAT placement, you'll locate that you will get much, far more from it if you proactively participate, as opposed to letting your male do all the job. The important point you must concentrate on is keeping your clitoris in close contact with both your male's pubic bone and also the reduced part of his penis, to maintain it promoted as he drives backwards and forwards. A wonderful way to maintain get in touch with is to wrap your legs around the back of your guy's legs as well as pull on your own into him.

You'll discover that you obtain even more out of the Coital Alignment Technique if you get into a good rhythm with your man, where you rock backwards and forwards as he drives backwards and forwards.

Guy roles

Your man is going to be thrusting up and down downwards as well as upwards (directly towards the mattres) when performing the Coital Alignment Technique placement. This is completely the opposite to missionary position, when your male is embedding as well as out in a primarily horizontal setting.

When doing the CAT with you, he won't be propelling that deeply, as part of his penis will certainly be outdoors your vaginal area. Instead, he requires to concentrate on remaining in contact with your clitoris virtually the entire time and also entering into a rhythm where you are both rocking to and fro while he is just carrying out little drives each time he rocks backward and forward.

The Coital Alignment Technique can be actually intimate. Try looking deep into your man's eyes and also rubbing his arms/back while he is penetrating you.

Tips

- The Coital Alignment Technique can feel great for you, however commonly your man might not get a lot from it.

- If you like clitoral stimulation during sex, then you will like the CAT sex position as your man will certainly remain in constant contact with your clit.

- If your man has a really brief penis, then he may have a bumpy ride executing the Coital Alignment Technique appropriately without frequently eloping.

- You may find the CAT frustrating as well as may not at first get anything out of it, however prior to surrendering on it, play around with a little various positions to see if they are more pleasurable for you. Try placing a cushion or pillow under your hips. Attempt obtaining your male to curve his back. Attempt shaking in a much more round movement as opposed to simply backwards and forwards.

6f. Cowboy Sex Position

The cowboy setting appears really comparable to the cowgirl position. That's because it is. Other than that the cowboy setting is the precise contrary to the cowgirl position. When carrying out the cowboy placement, the man is on top and also you are relaxing on your back.

All you truly require to do is exist there with both of your legs together. Your male then straddles you so that his legs are either side of you and his bottom is resting on your legs. Your male will require to bring his penis to enter you. To aid him originally permeate you, you can elevate your hips. Relying on what's most comfy and gives one of the most excitement for both of you, your male can then change himself either forwards or backwards.

The wonderful thing about the Cowboy sex placement is that it can supply a tighter feel for your guy.

Girl roles

When you are in the cowboy placement, you don't require to do a lot in all. You simply require to exist back and also take pleasure in the trip! Your male might find it quite challenging to first enter you. If he does, after that all you need to do is to spread your legs (which can be quite hard with your guy straddling you). You can additionally try lifting your hips upwards to bring your vagina closer to his penis. It's finest to permit your man to push his penis downwards to enter you. If you pull it downwards yourself, you have to be careful not to draw also difficult in case you mistakenly hurt him.

Man roles

Your guy will be doing mostly all of the work in the cowboy setting. He will certainly be doing all the thrusting. He can transform the angle of entry by leaning either forwards or in reverse while ahead (and bringing his hips either forwards or in reverse).

You can use your hands to aid manage rapid as well as deep your guy permeates you in the Cowboy setting.

Ensure to let him understand what placement really feels ideal.

When your man remains in the cowboy placement, he can, if placed correctly offer fairly a great deal of stimulation to your clitoral hood and also a little above it with his pubic bone.

Tips

- Your guy requires a bit of 'penis flexibility' to do the cowboy. This is due to the angles entailed. Your man will certainly have his penis strained downwards while permeating you, unless he is leaning right over you.

- The cowboy is fantastic if you like shallow penetration (or if your man is well put up). Since of the angles entailed, this is.

- Because your legs are with each other, this placement will certainly really feel a little tighter than the normal missionary setting.

6g. Criss Cross Sex Position

The Criss Cross sex position is a great little variant of many sex positions like The Playing Of the Cello. If you desire to offer your guy a tighter feeling during sex, the Criss Cross is excellent.

The Criss Cross position is a terrific variant of the Playing Of the Cello as it will feel tighter for your man.

To do it, you require to lay down on your back on either a table or a bed. You require to increase your legs so that they are directing towards the ceiling. Your guy will be standing up right for the Criss Cross. He needs to currently enter you. Once he does, maintain your legs as straight as possible as well as gradually cross them. You'll discover that it's easiest to cross your legs at your ankles. Crossing your legs will certainly make your vaginal area really feel method tighter to your man, the more you cross them, the tighter you will certainly come to be. The easiest position to have your legs in is to place them as much as his neck to make sure that one leg is on either side of it.

Girl roles

You'll discover that it's tough to do a lot at all when you are in the Criss Cross. Crossing your legs while on your back is quite immobilizing. What you can do is maintain changing exactly how much over you cross your legs till you discover a position that both your man as well as you take pleasure in.

If you place a pillow or padding under your hips/waist/butt, you will certainly find it easier as well as extra comfy to aim your legs in the direction of the ceiling.

Guy roles

Your guy is going to be doing all the embedding the Criss Cross placement. He can also aid you to cross your legs. Among the excellent features of the Criss Cross is that your man can easily get your legs before him to permeate you with a great deal even more force. If you are flexible enough, he can additionally lean right over you and also bed your legs backwards over you.

However the Criss Cross is not all about your male being 'dominant' or 'fucking you hard'. You'll both discover that it's actually wonderful to just try some fast but truly shallow infiltration also.

Tips

- Although your male is not right ahead you, he has the majority of the control, making it a wonderful position for those that like their male to take charge during sex.

- Your guy can cross your legs for you, however ensure he does not cross them too far and also hurt you!

- For strong, deep drives order the end of the bed/table with your hands to maintain on your own in position and also obtain your guy to hold onto your legs.

6h. Cross Sex Position

The Cross sex placement is precisely as it seems. When executing it with your man, your bodies will certainly be making the form of a cross. In numerous ways it's like the opposite of the X Marks The Spot position.

While the Cross setting is not exactly the most satisfying placement, it's still enjoyable to explore it.

Executing the Cross is easy. You just require to lie down on your stomach as well as your male will get on top of you. However you will certainly be lying with your feet by the end of the bed and also your head at the top of the bed by the pillows. Your male will certainly by lying with his feet on 1 side of the bed and also his directly the other side of the bed. By doing this, your 2 bodies will certainly develop a cross shape. Your male will certainly likewise be on his belly, encountering the bed and then entering you.

Woman roles

When in the Cross position, you will not really be doing a whole lot. The Cross is a little awkward which suggests that the most you can do is just returned against your male. His waistline will be resting on top of yours which indicates that you can delicately massage therapy it be getting to backwards. You can also get to over his butt with your hand as well as gently massage his testicles while he is permeating you.

Man roles

Your man will certainly be doing most of the operate in the Cross position. He will certainly locate it easier to thrust in as well as out if he lies somewhat on his side encountering in your instructions. Doing this takes a lot of the stress off his penis.

Your man may originally find it quite awkward in the Cross position, yet if he balances on his elbows as well as knees he will certainly have a little bit much more utilize for permeating you.

Tips

A great deal have stated that they did not particularly enjoy this sex position. Because this placement is simply not that intimate, the primary reason is. You aren't making much contact with each other.

You might discover the Cross to be a lot a lot more pleasurable if you alter your position somewhat to make sure that your guy's face and also shoulders are closer to your face and shoulders.

Try the cross with your man on either side. Some favor one side far more than the various other.

Don't fail to remember to try the Cross for anal sex.

Remarks

The Cross is an additional one of those sex positions that pairs are frequently eager to attempt merely since it looks 'different' or a little 'around'. Do not let this fool you. I have actually never ever obtained much pleasure from the Cross, also when attempting the variation.

6i. Deckchair Sex Position

Moving from Missionary or the Coital Alignment Technique to the Deckchair setting is very easy!

The deckchair is a fantastic male on the top sex placement that you must definitely try with your partner. Relocating into the deckchair position from regular missionary is incredibly easy. You stay laying on your back, while your man gets onto his knees as well as sustains himself on his hands placed under your knees. When in the deckchair placement, you need to raise your upper hands in the air.

If you like, you can after that grab your guy's shoulders or waist and even start rubbing your clit in this position. The great thing about the deckchair is that it's not difficult for either of you to enter it. However on top of that, it likewise allows you to stimulate locations that don't normally obtain much pleasure throughout routine missionary.

Lady roles

When you remain in the deckchair position, you can relax as well as appreciate the ride if you like. If you are a lot more energetic, after that there is a couple of things that you can do. One is boosting your clitoris with your hand(s). You can likewise delicately stroke your guy's arms that are either side of you.

Most guys like having their back gently scratched when they are making love with their partner, while a couple of like getting their back scraped quite hard. You can scrape the sides of his back while resting, however if you put your arms under his, and then order his shoulders, you'll be able to scratch a lot even more of his back.

Male roles

When your are lying down, you may find it tough to alter the angle at which your guy is penetrating you. Nonetheless, it's extremely simple for your male to alter his angle of access. A lot of the time, he will be leaning over you, resting on his hands. Yet he can likewise lean back quite a good bit till he finds an area that you both really take pleasure in.

When he's leaning truly far back, he'll locate that it's useful to grab on to your upper legs. This will also allow him to thrust with a lot more power if he holds them tight. In this position, he is not going to be able to provide your clitoris with much direct stimulation.

Tips

It's easy to do, also for an extended period without getting tired

It can take a little time to locate that 'ideal' position as well as rhythm.

If you still cannot find a truly pleasurable spot when in the deckchair placement, attempt putting a pillow under your lower back/hips/waist to raise it up as well as permit more angles.

You don't require super adaptability to do it.

If you or your guy like it hard and also deep, then you will discover that when he leans back as well as clinch your upper legs, he can fuck you truly hard.

Comments

I actually like the deckchair, particularly because it's so very easy to transition to from when I am having normal missionary, however likewise since you don't need to be too adaptable or stress on your own too much to do it for a long period of time.

6j. Deep Impact Sex Position

The Deep Impact placement is extremely comparable to the Criss Cross setting. It obtains its name from the reality that you can have extremely deep penetrative sex with your guy. It's likewise easy to have enthusiastic, also rough sex with you in this position.

If they are starting to become uneasy), you require to exist down on your back in this position and factor your legs in the direction of the ceiling (you can bend them. Your male will certainly get on his knees, upright, facing in the direction of you. He can either be on the flooring, less than you or on the bed. You require to relax your legs on his shoulders, one on each. He then orders you by your thighs and also holds you securely while he thrusting into you.

Your male can get your legs in the Deep Impact sex position so that he can penetrate you with more force.

Lady roles
You require to let your man do most of the job as it's a position for him to feel dominant in when you are in the Deep Impact position. If your male is kneeling on the floor as well as you go to the edge of the bed, then you can order the side of the bed as well as pull on your own in towards him with each drive.
Your guy will not be providing much stimulation to your clitoris in the Deep Impact position, so you can use your hands to masturbate yourself rather.

Male roles
Your man has a simple and really straightforward job in the Deep Impact position. He simply needs to embeded and out. That's it! He can get your legs to provide him more take advantage of if he wants to thrust harder. He can likewise slightly lean over you to dominate you more and change his angle. If he wants, he can lean in reverse and increase your waist from the bed.
He can experiment with how high he is by bringing his knees either closer together or even more apart if he is on his knees on the bed.

In the Deep Impact position, your man remains in control. If he wants to truly control you in this position, then he can lean right over you, continuing your legs, pinning you to the bed.

Tips
The Deep Impact is wonderful for rough, enthusiastic sex with your man. Yet often people get a little carried away as well as it can come to be extra excruciating than fun for you. If your man does obtain a little carried away, after that ensure to tell him. Wonderful sex is about 2 people appreciating themselves. It's not just about him enjoying, while you lie there awkward.

The Deep Impact is equally as great for anal sex as it is for vaginal sex.

Instead of getting you by the legs, he can order you by the arms as well as use them to draw you in.

Remarks

I find the Deep Impact position to be actually satisfying. It produces a terrific modification from slower, a lot more sensual sex. It's not something that I would advise for every time you have sex,

6k. Down Stroke Sex Position

The Down Stroke sex position resembles the Pile Driver in several methods, however it's not as severe which is just one of the reasons why it's more preferred than the Pile Driver. When he gets his thrusting right, one of the terrific things concerning the Down Stroke is that your man supplies a whole lot of excitement to your G-Spot.

When performing the Down Stroke, you require to start by pushing your back on the edge of your bed or couch with your legs increased in the air, aiming towards the ceiling like in the Deep Impact position. Your male will certainly be standing and also encountering you. He needs to order your legs and draw you up and also towards him so that he can enter you while standing up almost right. When he raises you up and in the direction of him, he will certainly be raising your waist straight off the bed so that just your top back as well as shoulders and also head are hing on the bed.

To aid relieve the stress on your head as well as neck, your male can partially lift you up.

Girl roles

You do not need to be totally straight/vertical when carrying out the Down Stroke.

When your man is holding you similar to this, you will certainly locate it actually hard to do a whole lot. You will certainly nonetheless be in a terrific position to masturbate. You can hold onto the side of the bed to pull yourself in with each stroke. Besides this, there actually isn't much for you to do besides holding eye contact with your man.

Guy roles

One of the most essential thing for your male in the Down Stroke position is not obtaining the angle right or exactly how he thrusts into you, it's how he holds you. Your man will have his hands wrapped around your thighs and will certainly be pulling you upwards. This can trigger a lot of stress on your skin which really feels actually aching (like it's concerning to rip) if he is not careful. So the first thing he needs to do is find a method to hold onto your thighs without injuring you.

After that he needs to focus on propelling in and also out once he has found a means to hold onto you. He requires to promote the top wall surface of your vaginal canal, that makes propelling horizontally ideal rather than propelling up and down.

Tips

- Don't allow your male to thrust too hard till he has actually found a way to keep you without harming you.
- The Down Stroke is a terrific position for having anal sex in, that makes it a lot easier for you to finger or masturbate on your own throughout it.

- Your male should do a little experimentation with how high he need to stand until he discovers a truly great position that you both delight in.

- If your male doesn't want to frequently hold you upright in the Down Stroke, after that you can fold a quilt or make use of several paddings put under your aware of take your weight.

6l. Drill Sex Position

The Drill sex position virtually appears to be a mix of both Missionary position and the Coital Alignment Technique. This means that it really feels terrific and also it's quite simple to carry out too!

The most effective method to start carrying out the Drill is to currently be in the Missionary position, which means that you should be pushing your back with your legs open. Your male needs to get on top of you, encountering you. When carrying out regular Missionary or the CAT sex position with your guy, you will have your legs on the bed, however this is where the Drill is various. Instead of having your legs hinge on the bed, you require to raise them and also cover them around your guy's midsection. To keep them wrapped around his waist, cross your ankle joints behind his back. This will certainly assist you to hold him and draw yourself right into him.

Locking your legs behind his back will certainly help to pull your guy in better for more forceful thrusting.

Lady roles
You'll find that the Drill position really feels a great deal much better than typical Missionary as your clitoris obtains promoted more together with the infiltration being much deeper. The first time you try it, you could discover it a little unpleasant to cover your legs around your male. Don't fret about this in any way. Just try it as well as you'll see that your guy will not mind having your legs around him. A lot of like it a great deal!

You can utilize your legs to gently pull your male in with each stroke. You'll discover it less complicated to draw him in towards you if you cover them around his butt rather than his waist. To make the Drill extra intimate as well as close feeling, make sure to wrap your arms around your guy's neck/back as well.

Male roles
Your man does not need an entire bunch of technological capability in the Drill position. It's just like routine Missionary. He can embeded and also out as regular. Or he can attempt getting closer and also grinding up and down on you to give you more clitoral satisfaction. While in addition to you, your guy has the choice of either supporting himself on his hands above you or obtaining closer to you by hing on his joints. He can even cover his arms around your back and over your shoulders for even more intimacy.

In numerous methods, the drill is rather similar to regular Missionary. You can likewise wrap your hands around your man's neck and also pull him in towards you to kiss him.

Tips

A number of trainees discussed that they were reluctant to squeeze with their legs tightly together in case they hurt their guy. The fact is you won't (unless he has some unusual, uncommon kidney condition). Unless you are a body building contractor, you will not ever hurt him. It will really feel actually wonderful for him, as if you are holding him more detailed.

If your male is well installed and also has a lengthy penis, then you might locate the infiltration to be unpleasant as well as well deep. Try putting a pillow in between your and his legs to quit him from going so deep if this is the instance.

Remarks

The Drill is a fantastic position for all couples to make use of as it instantly makes sex more intimate as well as it's so straightforward to do. It's likewise among those positions that your male does not require to know much about. You can stun him with it the next time your are both having sex in the Missionary position.

6m. Exposed Eagle Sex Position

The Exposed Eagle sex position is one of the hardest placements to execute It requires an excellent degree of flexibility and also strength. If you do not have these, then you are both in for a quite aching time!

As you can see from the demo, you need to have a suitable degree of flexibility to manage the Exposed Eagle comfortably.

The most convenient means to enter the Exposed Eagle position is to begin in the Cowgirl position. This means that you require to on top of your male with your knees on either side of him. You then require to lie backwards till your back is resting on your male's upper legs as well as knees while you are still on your knees. He can increase his knees if you aren't flexible enough so you are a lot more upright. Your man currently requires to raise his upper body to ensure that he is in a seated position. He can place his arms behind him to support himself or he can put them around your back.

Lady roles

When you remain in the Exposed Eagle, you will undoubtedly be feeling very revealed, but you will also discover it difficult to in fact do much. Your legs will certainly be really immobile as well as your back will certainly be curved.

Your hands will be complimentary though. You can make use of the se to rub on your own around.

This is as much for you as it is for your man. You can likewise scrub his legs or arms.

Guy roles

Your man's very first top priority is to make sure that you are comfortable and having a good time. If this is your first time attempting the Exposed Eagle, after that your legs might feel sore and a little 'squeezed'. He requires to supply you with adequate support to your back.

Your guy will be in the excellent position to lean forward to kiss and also draw your busts if you discover that you can arch your bike right back. He can use his hands to massage and caress them instead if your man finds it uncomfortable to lean forward.

Tips

If you are serious about it, you should attempt stretching beforehand. You ought to concentrate on extending your quads and also your guy must focus on extending his back.

To do the Exposed Eagle correctly, you are expected to maintain your legs bent. But sex isn't regarding rules and guidelines! If you are not that flexible, then forget about flexing your knees as well as just align them out. This takes most of the pain/stress out of it.

This position is great for anal sex too, but like with most positions, I always advise that you try vaginal.

Comments

Directly I am not the biggest follower of the Exposed Eagle position. For me, sex is about shedding yourself as well as having a good time. I am not that versatile therefore the Exposed Eagle feels a lot more like job to me than fun.

6n. Hang Loose Sex Position

The Hang Loose is a really very easy to execute variation of routine Missionary position. You do not have to be a gymnast or 'Stretch Armstong' to perform it with your male.

The Hang Loose sex position is really similar to Missionary, but a lot more 'cost-free' as you can hang your head right over the edge of the bed.

To get into the Hang Loose position with your man, simply start off in the regular Missionary position with him, yet rather than lying with your heads by where the pillows are and also your feet near completion of the bed, both lie throughout the bed. Existing throughout the bed will certainly offer both of you much less room. To overcome this, position yourself to make sure that your head and part of your shoulders are hanging over the edge of the bed. Your man will certainly likewise be hanging over the bed, so he will require to extend his arms outwards and also place his hands on the ground to support himself.

The Hang Loose got it's name from the fact that you are both hanging over the side of your bed.

Girl roles
Like I've already said, the Hang Loose is simply a small variant of regular Missionary. As you are existing over the edge of the bed, it allows you to extra easily curve your back to aid create a somewhat various angle of access for your man.

You'll locate that having your head and part of your shoulders hang over the edge of the bed does not allow you to do a lot. This is the entire point of the Hang Loose. It allows you to 'let go' and allow your man take control.

Male roles
Your male will be embedding and out like he typically does during the Missionary position. He can likewise grind up against you also. For some pairs this can really feel almost similar to normal old Missionary position. This is why I suggest that your male try slightly various placements, like the permeating you while he is on his knees as well as your legs impend, similar to in the Deep Impact position or the Coital Alignment Technique position if he can obtain himself into the right position while hanging over the side of the bed.

You can wrap your arms around his midsection, around his back or around his neck. You can also try wrapping your legs around his back and locking your ankle joints together like in the Drill position.

Tips

When having regular Man-On-Top sex with your man, - It's a great (and easy) position to do if you want to change things up.

- If you like, you can outstretch your arms behind on your own and place your hands on the floor to aid keep on your own stabilized in the Hang Loose position. This also arches your back.

- The Hang Loose is a fantastic position if you like your male taking control throughout sex.

If you have a bad back or neck, do not perform the Hang Loose position.

Remarks

I love the Hang Loose position. There are tons of variants of it (based on other Man-On-Top sex placements) which implies that you will not obtain burnt out for a long time.

60. Italian Hanger Sex Position

The Italian Hanger is a fantastic sex position for striking your G-Spot while likewise having a great 'exposed' and also slightly passive feeling to it. It's extremely simple to transfer from the normal Missionary postion right into the Italian Hanger. You just need to rest on your back.

While your man is having normal missionary sex, he then requires to reach his knees and also bring them rather near to you, which will require your legs apart. He then needs to put his hands under your bum and hips and lift them up when he is on his knees. To help him elevate your bottom as well as hips, flex your knees and also plant your feet on the bed. This will certainly allow you to push you hips/waist into the air.

You can plant your feet on the bed to assist keep your waist raised.

Lady roles

You need to help to keep your waist elevated otherwise your mans arms are going to quickly tire when you are in the Italian Hanger position. This is normally rather easy, however if you locate that you are obtaining tired/weak from maintaining your waist raised, then try placing a couple of pillows/cushions under your back to keep it elevated.

When doing the Italian Hanger with your man, if you want him to make even more contact with the upper wall of your vaginal area (G-Spot), then try arching your back a little, while also pushing back onto him.

When you remain in this position, your man isn't mosting likely to be reaching your clit, so if you want, you can supply on your own with some hand-operated stimulation utilizing your hands.

Man roles

Your man is going to be doing the majority of the operate in the Italian Hanger position. He will certainly be embedding as well as out of you. He will certainly additionally have his hands on your waistline (or under it), maintaining it elevated. Your guy will certainly have a great deal of control over the angles he enters you at. By leaning back, he can supply even more pressure as well as stimulation to your G-Spot. But if he leans onward, over you, he will certainly penetrate you much deeper.

He can grab your arms or hands to pull you towards him with each thrust if he wants to penetrate you with more power.

You can additionally attempt using pillows under your midsection if you do not enjoy your male holding you.

He can put his arms under your waist and lift you up so that your back and head are taken right off the bed if your man is strong enough. This position can make you feel actually complimentary as well as revealed, with your guy in nearly complete control.

Tips

Pillows as well as pillows are your pals. There is no factor in both you and also your male getting truly tired maintaining your waist boosted. The remedy: Put a few pillows/cushions under your lower back to provide you some assistance.

A little adaptability is needed.

Don't fail to remember to maintain your knees bent as well as feet on the bed to aid keep your midsection elevated.

Try putting your hands on the headboard/wall behind you and push back onto your guy with each of his thrusts for deeper and more powerful penetration.

Comments

The Italian Hanger is a great sex positon that is relatively very easy to carry out as well as change to. It's likewise a fairly dominant position for your guy. You may discover in the beginning, that it's not that satisfying. Keeping varying how much your arch your back and raise your waist/hips until you find a spot that feels great if this is the case

6p. Launching Pad Sex Position

The Launch Pad sex position is super enjoyable and has the wonderful feeling of your man being on top of you, dominating you.

In the Lauchpad position, you can use your feet to push back versus your guy's breast to manage exactly how deep you take him.

To get into the Launch Pad position, you need to start by resting on your back with your guy penetrating while on his knees facing you. You then need to lift your legs upwards and also bring your knees to your breast. You can after that relax your feet on your guys chest. Your guy can after that lean over you which will permit you to easily raise your hips permitting really deep penetration. Relocating into the Launch Pad position from a position like the Deep Impact is a breeze.

Girl roles

When you are resting on your back in the Launch Pad position, your male will certainly appear like he has the majority of the control. You will actually be the one who has most control. Because your feet are on his upper body you can manage how deep and also fast he permeates you.

If you find having your feet on your man's upper body to be uncomfortable, then you can always simply put them on either side of him or both away of him. If you do, it may look more like you remain in the anvil or deckchair placements though. As your hips will be raised a little in this position, it's ideal for masturbating yourself to assist bring yourself to climax.

Guy roles

Sex in the Launch Pad position is truly straightforward for your man. He just requires to embeded and out. However if you want him to strike a certain spot or fuck you at 'that ideal angle' in the Launch Pad position, then he will certainly require to adjust himself a little from leaning right over you to leaning quite far back until he locates an actually wonderful angle. You can aid regulate just how much he leans over you utilizing your feet. Apart from embedding as well as out and adjusting the angle he penetrates you at, there is not a lot else your male needs to do.

Tips

Anal sex is just as simple in the Launch Pad position.

Make certain that both of your share the workload. Your man can embedded to you and you can press him back out with your feet.

Some men get a little over-enthusiastic in this position and lean so far over you, that they start to injure your legs. If this starts to take place, ensure to allow your male know.

If you are not flexible enough to carry out the Launch Pad, then just attempt placing your feet sideways rather than on his chest.

Tips
The Launch Pad is a terrific position. It truly enjoyable and satisfying for both of you and also it's fairly easy to execute.

6q. Missionary Sex Position

The missionary position is one of the most typical sex positions in the world. The reason for it's popularity is that it's easy to carry out, it really feels terrific and also many people already understand it.

The Missionary position is wonderful for raising intimacy during sex & making deep eye contact with your male.
The image over is how the missionary position is executed with your companion. You require to lie on your back, with your legs open. The man then places himself in addition to you to ensure that his legs remain in between your own. The man can steady himself by relaxing his weight on his elbow joints which he places either side of you. He can additionally relax part of his weight on you, but need to be careful to see to it that it's not uneasy for you. Ensure to inform him if it is. When you are concerning to sex in the missionary position, you might discover that you require to guide your guy's penis into your vaginal area.

Girl roles
The missionary position is extremely simple and does not require much agility or versatility at all, so it's appropriate for any ages. For the man to execute it, he merely needs to propelled his penis in and out of your vaginal area. While propelling his penis in and out is absolutely pleasant for you, you will certainly find that it's much more enjoyable for you if he can move his hips up and down at the same time so that his pubic bone can apply pressure onto and around your clitoris.
In this position, the man has a good degree of control on exactly how deep he permeates you and well as how quickly.

Man roles
When you are making love in the missionary position with your man, you may feel that because he is on top, that he's the one in control. You'll be stunned to learn that you in fact additionally have an excellent degree of control over exactly how deep he penetrates you along with how much stimulation your clitoris gets.
When your guy gets on top of you, you can cover your arms around his neck or head, or alternatively you can 'hook' your arms beneath his and also order his back so that you can draw on your own down onto his penis for a little much deeper penetration.
To Stimulate Your Clitoris: If you desire him to boost your clitoris more than he currently is, then all you require to do is grind it against his pubic bone on every thrust. It will certainly take a bit to obtain your rhythm, but once you do, it really feels impressive!

To Make Him Penetrate You Deeper: To obtain him to penetrate you much deeper when having missionary sex is really easy. All you need to do is raise your boosts. Keeping them elevated airborne will quickly tire you, so your best bet is to wrap them around your companion's back.

If you do not like covering your legs around your partner, but still wish for much deeper infiltration, after that you can put a cushion or padding under the small of your back/hips area. This will certainly boost your vaginal area as well as allow him to penetrate you more deeply without you have to raise your legs.

Throughout the Missionary position you can wrap you arms around his neck and pull him in to you to kiss him. Or you can reveal your sensual side by gently ordering his hair!

Why this position?

- It enables totally body call, raising affection and also nearness.
- It enables you to quickly kiss your companion on the lips throughout sexual intercourse which once again raises the sensation of intimacy as well as distance.

- Many girls locate it exciting that their male remains in a slightly dominant position when on top of the m. Some claim that they feel like he is pinning them to the bed and is 'in control'.
- When carried out appropriately it is unbelievably pleasurable for both you as well as your guy, without either of you having to carry out any type of sex-related gymnastics that some sex positions usually call for.

Comments
If you haven't had sex sometimes in the past, then you'll locate that the missionary position is really simple to execute. Among one of the most underrated facets of it is that you have a huge degree of control regarding how deep you take your man.

You should likewise keep in mind that during the Missionary position, your male can hinge on his joints rather than his hands.

6r. Missionary 180 Sex Position

The Missionary 180 Sex Position resembles a mix of both the Betty Rocker position as well as routine Missionary. For your guy it will certainly call for a fair bit of flexibility in his penis to execute it.

The Missionary 180 position can produce a wonderful adjustment, but your male requires a good little bit of 'penile adaptability' to execute it easily.

To get involved in the Missionary 180 position, you initially need to start by relaxing on your back with you legs rather spread out. Your guy will after that rest on top of you. But rather than existing face-to-face, he will certainly be lying head-to-toe with his legs expanded so that they are resting on the bed on either side of you. He after that needs to slowly and also meticulously push his penis downwards so that he can enter you. This will place a lot of stress on the suspensory ligaments in his penis so he requires to be added mindful while doing this.

Lady roles

Firstly, it's actually crucial not to pull his penis with your hands when he is entering into the Missionary 180 position. You don't intend to hurt him! It's a good suggestion to use your hands to aid direct him inside you.

When he is inside you, attempt to stay fairly still while your male obtains comfy. You can attempt to gradually propelled back versus him when he is comfy thrusting right into you after a minute or 2. You can put your hands on his butt to assist him locate an angle that you both really delight in as well as give some added thrust.

Guy roles

Like I have actually currently been stating, your male needs to be quite careful when checking out the Missionary 180 position. He can actually harm himself if he's not careful. If he does really feel an extreme pressure on his penis throughout sex, then he ought to pull out and also attempt a various lovemaking position.

While carrying out the Missionary 180, all your male requires to do is just thrust backwards and forwards.

When performing the Missionary 180, you are in the ideal position to play with your guy's ass as well as spheres!

Tips

It can be actually unpleasant for your guy in this position, so don't worry if you cannot pull it off, there are 100 ' s of various other excellent sex positions for you to attempt.

A fantastic means to see if your male will be able to execute the Missionary 180 is to first try the Betty Rocker position with him as it's almost the same, yet you can take the pressure off his penis extra easily.

Comments

To be flawlessly sincere, I included the Missionary 180 position since it's various and exotic, yet I don't directly appreciate it much at all.

6s. Pirates Bounty Sex Position

The Pirates Bounty sex position resembles a cross in between the Deep Impact position as well as the Leg Glider position

The Pirate's Bounty position is a wonderful little variation on the likes of the Sandwich or the Playing Of the Cello.

To perform it with your man, you require to begin by pushing your back like you would for regular Missionary sex with your legs open. Your man after that needs to kneel down beside your vagina, facing you with his legs spread out apart to make sure that he can lower himself down and enter you. He then needs to grab among your legs as well as slowly bring it up to make sure that it's practically aiming in the direction of the ceiling. He can then rest it on his shoulder as well as placed his arm around it.

Girl roles

The Pirates Bounty is extremely comparable to the Deep Impact position in that you don't have much to do whatsoever. You can lower your hand to help you provide on your own much more enjoyment if you like. A straightforward method to make the Pirates Bounty a whole lot a lot more intimate is to maintain eye contact with your guy.

You require to let your male know if he is placing as well much stress on your leg if you are not that flexible. If he is, try bending to lower the pressure it.

Male roles

Your male will certainly be propelling right into you as he generally would in the Deep Impact position. This implies that he will have one arm twisted around your elevated leg and his various other holding onto your leg that's hing on the bed to make sure that he can powerfully embedded as well as out of you.

He won't be able to spread his legs that much if you're male is not that versatile. This indicates he will require to draw you as much as him to permeate you fully. If you are flexible enough, after that your person can likewise lean over you while you are

Having sex to make it feel like he is controlling you.

You can use your hands on his belly as well as waistline to help manage just how deep you take him.

Tips

Try alternating between which leg is elevated as well as which leg is decreased. Numerous have located that they slightly choose having one leg elevated as well as the other on the bed.

If you intend to feel your man even deeper, after that cover your leg that isn't elevated around your sweetheart's back and pull him in towards you with each drive.

If you like quickly, enthusiastic sex with your guy, after that he can place both arms around your elevated leg and hold on to it tightly, enabling him to propelled really hard.

Comments

I take into consideration the Pirates Bounty sex position to be a variation of various other sex positions. It's not some insane, strange new position that will certainly give you radically various sensations as well as enjoyments. However it is fantastic for transforming things up with your man in bed. When it comes to getting better at sex, and that's one of the most important things. Injecting and also trying brand-new things variation into your sex life.

6t. The Playing Of the Cello Sex Position

The Playing of the Cello sex position is a really enjoyable one. Because your guy will look a little like he is playing the cello with your legs, the factor that it's called the Playing of the Cello is.

To do it, you require to push your back and also raise your legs to ensure that they are aiming towards the ceiling. Your man is then located upright, on his knees as well as enters you while encountering you. You then require to rest both of your legs on simply among his shoulders. Your man after that covers one arm around your feet as well as lower leg, while covering his other arm around your thighs, which makes him resemble he's playing the cello with your legs, for this reason the name.

When your guy holds your legs during the Play of the Cello position, he can get even more utilize to permeate you deeply with more power!

Woman roles
When you are in the Playing of the Cello lovemaking position, your male will certainly be doing almost all of the job. All you need to do is just enjoy the trip. Fortunately your hands will be complimentary the entire time. This means that you can satisfaction yourself by hand, while you're male embed and out.

Man roles
Your man is mosting likely to be doing virtually every one of the operate in The Playing Of the Cello position. As he is holding both your upper and lower legs, it implies that he can extremely quickly hold you ready or draw you towards him for much deeper, harder thrusts. If he desires, he can lean in reverse, while still holding your legs limited or lean forwards pressing your legs on top of you to change his angle of entrance.

Tips
This is a great position for your guy to take a lot of control as well as 'bang you truly hard' as one pupil put it.

When you man leans in reverse, he places more pressure on your G-Spot, which will promote it a whole lot even more.

A few pairs said that they located this position to be extremely hot and also attractive, however it had not been particularly intimate, as you are not very close together unless your man is leaning right over you.

You do not need to maintain your legs directly in this position. Rather, you can flex your knees to take the strain off your hamstrings and bottom.

Remarks

I really appreciate the Playing Of the Cello sex position. It's wonderful for enthusiastic sex when I'm with a girl that appreciates deep as well as tough drives and a small feeling of being exposed.

6u. Angle Sex Position

They always appear to never ever have listened to of it when I explain the Right Angle sex position to individuals. The thing is, it's a really easy to perform position and doesn't require massive quantities of versatility.

Don't worry too much concerning keeping your legs perfectly directly or placing your feet together during the Right Angle position like in the picture. Relax and appreciate it!
You require to start by setting on your back and pointing your feet in the direction of the ceiling. You don't need to stress way too much about keeping your legs perfectly right. Following your man needs to sit down on the bed with his legs open. He should be encountering you and sitting down on the bed just listed below your vaginal area with his legs before him on either side of your body. Your guy then requires to grab your legs as well as raise you up and also in the direction of him. He can then penetrate you.
The Right Angle gets its name from the truth that both of you will certainly be making a 90 degree angle (best angle) with your bodies.

Lady roles
As you will certainly be resting in the Right Angle position, you might find it a little tough to be and also move that energetic during sex. Do not fret, there is still a ton of things that you can do to make it fun for both of you
The easiest thing to do is to keep eye contact with your male while he is fucking you. This will assist to raise the affection. You can likewise hold onto his legs that get on either side of you to offer you a little leverage to gently return onto your man. One of the coolest aspects of the Right Angle position is that you can utilize a vibe to assist you orgasm during sex.

Male roles
Your man might additionally initially locate the Right Angle position to be uncomfortable. When resting down with his legs extended, this is generally due to the reality that he will certainly find it difficult to propel. There are 2 ways around this:
1) He can place his hands underneath you butt/waist/hips and lift you backwards and forwards or get your legs as well as use them to lift you backwards and forwards.
2) He can grab hold of your arms as well as pull you in to him as you grind on him.

Tips
Don't really feel that you require to maintain your legs right. See to it to bend them.
It's a wonderful beginning position when you want to attempt something brand-new in the bed room as it's not that complex and also you don't require to stretch as well as flex your limbs.
The Right Angle position is excellent for either anal or genital sex.

A fun variation of the best angle position. Called the Straight sex position, it's a fairly comparable to the Tug of Love.

Comments
Like I already said, the Right Angle is an easy to carry out position and also it feels excellent. For some reason it simply hasn't seen to have ever caught on like the Missionary position and also Doggy Style has. I highly suggest that you attempt it out with your male quickly if you have actually never attempted it previously.

6v. Sandwich Sex Position

The Sandwich sex position is a little bit like a mix of both the Drill position and also the Viennese Oyster position. It calls for a little bit of strength and also versatility on your part.

To do the Sandwich, just rest on your back as well as let your male permeate while he's on top as he normally would when doing the Missionary. Instead of simply resting your legs on the bed like you normally would, bring them in the direction of on your own while maintaining them open. Your man's arms ought to usually be around your shoulders on the bed, however he is now going to decrease them to make sure that he can place one under each of your knees and also assist you to raise them upwards to alter the angle that he's permeating you at.

Carrying out the Sandwich position conveniently with your male needs an excellent level of versatility.

Lady roles
You need to make certain that you are fairly flexible before you attempt the Sandwich position with your male.

You ought to avoid it if you have a weak reduced back or the back of your knee conveniently obtains sore.

Then all you have to stress about is maintaining your legs raised without it being also uncomfortable once you are pleased to do the Sandwich with your male. If it is, see to it to inform your male. The Sandwich is an extremely dominant position for your male, so there is not a great deal you can do. You can utilize your hands to scrub his back and also shoulders. You can additionally kiss him.

Guy roles
Your guy will have virtually complete control in the Sandwich position, so he needs to make sure that you are appreciating it as much as he is. He will certainly be keeping your legs held upwards towards your breast utilizing his arms behind your knees which can feel really revealing and also be an actual turn on for some.

Besides this, he will certainly be thrusting in and out of you and grinding backwards and forwards on you also. While doing this, he is additionally in the best position to kiss you on the neck, cheeks as well as mouth.

If you like feeling your guy control you, then you will like the Sandwich!

Tips

The Sandwich is great for those of you that enjoy clitoral excitement from your man. Because of lifting your legs with his arms during sex, he will certainly have the ability to give wonderful excitement to your clit with his pubic bone.

A couple of have actually claimed that they only appreciate the Sandwich for a couple of mins before it's also sore on the backs of the ir legs.

Remarks

The Sandwich sex position is among those positions that I'm not crazy about as it's a little awkward, but it's still wonderful to use from time to time to flavor points up.

6w. Pull Of Love Sex Position

To enter the Tug Of Love, your man first needs to relax on the bed on his back with his legs open. You then require to muffle top of him and let him enter you, with your legs on either side of him ahead you. Following you need to begin leaning in reverse till you are resting on the bed (put your arms behind you to reduce yourself down). Your head ought to be close to his feet. You can rest your legs on his chest or on either side of him, whichever is more comfy.

The Tug Of Love can be quite an awkward position, as you can see over!
Now that you are both relaxing, your guy ought to get your hands/arms to ensure that he can pull you in towards him.

Woman roles
When you initially try out the Tug Of Love position, you might find it to be a little odd and that it takes a little while to get utilized to. That's flawlessly regular.
You after that need to start focusing on grinding on your male when you are comfy. Just move your hips up-and-down as well as side-to-side while he is inside you. This is a lot harder when on your back, however it's still easier than propelling onto him. If your male is not holding your arms, you are also in an ideal position to start masturbating on your own while in the Tug Of Love position.

Man roles
Your man will also initially find it uncomfortable in the Tug Of Love, specifically since his penis will certainly be curved in reverse a little
When in the Tug Of Love position, your man will certainly be holding onto your hands/arms. He can pull himself truly snugly into you and then start grinding on you utilizing his hips or he can alternate how tightly he holds you. Your male can also propelled up and down in the Tug Of Love position. Your male requires to be cautious not to injure you in the Tug Of Love position. If your arms are beginning to obtain aching, then your man can hold onto your legs rather.

Remarks
I do not delight in the Tug Of Love position that much. Even though I am not a fan of it, I still think that it's worth trying out a couple of times to maintain things fascinating in the room.

6x. Success Sex Position

The Victory sex position is a fun modification from having sex in the Drill position or Missionary position. It's also great due to the fact that it's fairly easy to do as well!

You initially need to begin by lying on your back with your legs open as you normally would when your male is on top. Your male will certainly after that straddle you as he normally would throughout normal Missionary sex. Instead of wrapping your legs around him, you require to keep them open as well as aiming in the air in a 'V' form.

Now you may be thinking that you have to keep your legs in a best 'V' shape. You do not need to. If you did, you would find them getting weary actually quickly. So do not hesitate to flex them if they are getting aching.

When performing the Victory, don't worry about maintaining your legs directly. If you discover your legs burning out, you can rest them on his back, like in the Drill position.

Girl roles
The Victory position is one in which your man will be tackling a very leading function, while you will be in a more passive function. When doing the Victory position ... yet it's always great for him when you are, you do not need to be actually active!

The wonderful thing about the Victory position is that both of you will certainly be dealing with each other. Don't forget to make eye call with him. You can additionally place your hands around his neck and pull him in close for a kiss. Something a lot of individuals enjoy is for you to carefully run your hands backwards and forwards his back while he is thrusting right into you. If you like, you can additionally begin scrubbing your clitoris, aiding yourself to climax.

Man roles
For your man, the Victory position is really uncomplicated. He is doing fantastic if he just thrusts in and also out while on his knees. To make it much more enjoyable for you, he should try rotating in between thrusting in and also out of you and also grinding up against you. By grinding backwards and forwards on you (while inside you), he won't be offering you with as much vaginal stimulation, however he will certainly be able to provide a great deal more pressure/stimulation to your clitoral area.

Tips
- It's fantastic for those that like their male to have a great deal of control or to 'supervise' throughout sex.
- Anal sex is likewise feasible with the Victory.
- Depending on the angle of access, you can accomplish very deep penetration throughout the Victory position.

6y. Viennese Oyster Sex Position

The Viennese Oyster is fairly an unique position that requires you to have a huge amount of flexibility and suppleness. As you can see aware below, to perform it, you need to lay on your back. You then have to grab your legs and spread them while also pulling them in reverse.

As you can see, you need a great deal of flexibility to perform the Viennese Oyster with your man. It's a great suggestion to attempt something a little less laborious first like the Sandwich.

At some point you will certainly have drew them back until now that you knees will certainly be touching the bed (or practically touching it) on either side of you. You can after that put your arms in addition to your legs (at the rear of your knees) which will certainly keep your legs in place. If you locate this actually easy to do, you can experiment already placing your legs better back behind your head.

Your guy after that penetrates you while on his knees, just as he would when in the deckchair position.

Girl roles
Your legs will not be able to move a whole lot when you are executing the Viennese Oyster. One of the most you can do is either masturbate on your own or scrub your guy's chest.

Male roles
He requires to be added careful not to injure you if this is your very first time executing the Viennese Oyster with your man. When you start in this position, make sure that your guy goes slow-moving, mild as well as listens to your for responses. Then as soon as you are completely comfortable, he can get a little bit extra aggressive. He also has to be careful with his first couple of drives to make sure that he does not go too deep, which is very simple in this position.

As I have actually already claimed, your male is going to get on his knees. By relocating his knees closer or better far from you, he can change just how deep he goes as well as what angle he is penetrating you at. If you actually like clitoral stimulation throughout sex, then you'll need to offer it on your own, due to the fact that it's very tough for your guy to offer it with his pubic bone in this position.

Tips
- If you are not adaptable, then forget it.
- Even if you are flexible as well as can carry out the Viennese Oyster, you will possibly still find it extremely awkward.
- Warming up and doing some stretching first is a great idea and will make it much easier to do.

When he is on top of you, - Your guy has a huge quantity of control. If you like really feeling exposed and obtaining controlled and being submissive to him, this is great. He can actually 'extra pound you from above'.

- It's also wonderful if you like taking it really deep from him.

6z. X Marks The Spot Sex Position

The X Marks The Spot sex position is truly just a variation of the normal Missionary position. If you find that you are getting tired of Missionary and want something different yet similar, it's fantastic to attempt out.

This suggests that to execute it, you need to lay on your back while your man is on top. The X Marks The Spot position obtain's the 'X' part from the truth that your bodies will form an X when watched from above. If you are lying down on your back with your feet at the end of the bed and your head at the top of the bed where the cushions generally are, your guy will be existing throughout the bed, with his head by one side of the bed as well as his feet by the various other side of the bed.

While the X Marks the Spot Position is very easy and enjoyable to experiment with, many people have actually reported that it's not as satisfying as a lot of the various other positions in The Book.

Lady roles
When in the X Marks the Spot position, you will at first find it to be a little tough and also awkward. That should change after a few minutes. You'll locate that you can returned versus your guy just as you would certainly when doing normal Missionary. When thrusting back versus your guy, you won't get as much clitoral excitement as regular, so feel free to utilize your hands to give a little additional fun to aid you orgasm. And even take into consideration making use of a vibrator.

You can also keep your male's leg/butt and draw him down and right into you with each drive for more powerful penetration.

Guy roles
You male has a truly simple job in the X Marks the Spot position. All he requires to do is simply embeded and out. That's it.

If he likes, he can do a minor variation where he holds onto your arm with his arm closest to you to ensure that he can pull himself right into you with each thrust. Doing this can likewise alter the angle of entrance somewhat.

When performing the X Marks The Spot Position, you remain in the best position to spank your male. Great for spicing points up!

Tips
If you want to attempt it out, - It's actually very easy to change from routine Missionary to the X Marks The Spot position as well as back once again.
- Anal sex is practically difficult in the X Marks The Spot position.

Since there isn't much body get in touch with, - Many located that the X Marks The Spot position lacks affection.

Comments
I would not think about the X Marks The Spot position to be that great. It's not truly that intimate for pairs as you are both rarely touching each others bodies. Your heads are additionally extremely far apart which suggests that it's truly challenging to kiss each other also. I would certainly file the X Marks The Spot position under, 'Something brand-new to attempt' and not under 'truly intimate'.

Chapter 7. Pushing Your Stomach Sex Positions

Having sex while pushing your stomach is great if you are really exhausted and wish to relax. Making love with your guy while resting on your tummy can be intimate and also extremely peaceful or additionally, it can be quite vigorous, hot as well as sexy depending upon what type of mood you remain in. Bumper Cars Position, Irish Garden Position, Jockey Position, Rear Entry Position, Superwoman Position

7a. Bumper Cars Sex Position

The Bumper Cars sex position is a really unique one. Even the name is a little 'out there'. The interesting feature of the Bumper Cars position is that some consider it to be a full uniqueness.

To carry out the Bumper Cars position, your man is mosting likely to very first need to examine that his penis is adaptable sufficient. If he is standing directly, after that he requires to be able to point it straight downwards in the direction of the ground fairly conveniently prior to even attempting the Bumper Cars.

When he initially tries out the Bumper Cars position, your male needs to be mindful.

If your man has enough versatility, after that it's time to proceed! First you need to rest on your stomach on your bed, with your legs directly as well as open wide. After that your guy needs to lie down on his stomach facing in entirely the contrary direction with his legs straight and widen too. He then requires to turn around back towards you until his thighs are placed over your upper legs and also he can pull his penis so that it's directing towards your vagina. He slowly requirements to enter you, ensuring not to overstretch his penis.

Woman roles

You first need to be really still while your guy gets right into position as well as enters you when you are in the Bumper Cars position. You require to remain quite still until he is comfy thrusting in and also out when he does enter you. Once your guy is completely comfortable inside you, you can additionally start to gently gyrate your hips.

As this position doesn't allow for especially deep infiltration, don't bother doing any propelling on your own as it will certainly make him elope far more typically.

Male roles

Keep in mind: Even though this sex position looks unique, it does not imply that it's more enjoyable.

Your man's initial concern is making certain that he stays secure as well as doesn't unintentionally hurt himself by straining the suspensory ligaments in his penis. He needs to gradually propel in and also out when he is comfortable as well as certain. Whish's it! He can thrust by either moving his whole body or by just utilizing his hips.

Your guy should maintain readjusting his position till he locates something that fits for both of you.

Tips

When you are in this position, - Make sure that you begin out unbelievably gradually.

- If you enjoy having your feet rubbed or giving a foot massage during sex, then the Bumper Cars position is perfect for both you as well as your guy as your feet are right beside his hands and also vice-versa.

Due to the fact that the Bumper Cars looks actually unique doesn't suggest that it's even more satisfying than other sex positions, - Just. As a matter of fact a lot of couples and also students hate it.

Comments

While some individuals see the Bumper Cars position as being fairly similar to the Betty Rocker sex position, I don't. Personally not especially intimate (you face is about 5 feet far from your partners while performing it and also you are not also encountering each other!).

7b. Irish Garden Sex Position

The Irish Garden is a really interesting sex position. When a lot of couples see it first, they assume that it requires a crazy amount of flexibility. The reality is, it does not. It's in fact truly easy to do. Somehow the Irish Garden is fairly similar to the Betty Rocker position.

The Irish Garden position is truly simple to execute with your male, even though many have never ever tried it!

To enter into the Irish Garden position, your male requires to very first muffle the bed. He needs to have his back upright and straight. His legs need to be out in front of him and opened up relatively large.

If it makes it extra comfy for him, he can bend his knees. You then require to come down on all fours and reverse on your own in the direction of him. You will certainly have lower your midsection down onto your guy by straightening out your legs behind him (one on either side of his midsection). Currently reduced your head as well as shoulders onto the bed till they are resting on it.

Woman roles

In the Irish Garden position, you will certainly be practically lying down on your tummy while your man enters you. You'll find that in this position that your male can't propelled much, so you will be in charge of the thrusting.

You can use your aware of relocate on your own up and down on your man's penis in a rocking motion. When your knees are securely on the bed, you'll find this simpler to do. You can additionally get your man's lower legs with your hands to hold on your own in position.

But the Irish Garden is not concerning strenuous thrusting. It's a wonderful relaxing position for slower, extra sensual sex.

Male roles

Your man will find it tough to thrust right into you whatsoever. Instead, he can place his hands on your butt/hips/waist as well as carefully rock you to and fro.

In the Irish Garden, your guy is in the best position to scrub as well as massage your back. If he is not that versatile, after that he can lean back as well as use his arms to sustain himself or he can place some cushions under his back.

Tips

- If you intend to your guy to propelled into you, after that place your arms behind your back and also let your guy get your hands so that he can pull you in with each drive.

- If your guy is versatile, after that he can lean ahead and also push your back to make it really feel extra like a spooning position.

When watching TV/pornography with their guy, - Some enjoy this position.

- You can massage your male's feet when in this position.

Remarks

The Irish Garden position is great! It's simple as well as it's gives you a truly different angle of entry, which is ideal if you find yourself getting bored throughout sex.

7c. Jockey Sex Position

The Jockey sex position gets it's name from the basic reality that your male is going to resemble a jockey riding an equine when you are making love in this position

.

If you want to unwind while your guy does most of the work, then you will certainly enjoy the Jockey position.

To do the Jockey with your guy, you simply require to exist face down on your bed with your legs straight as well as with each other. Your man after that needs to straddle you with his knees on either side of your waist. He can then enter your either vaginally or anally and begin propelling. While he can lean onward like a jockey would certainly when riding a racehorse, he does not need to. He can even lean in reverse a little in the Jockey position. He can additionally lean right on top of you to ensure that it really feels more like you are spooning with him.

Girl roles

If you delight in being totally easy throughout sex, then you'll love the Jockey. It's the best position for continuing to be passive. All you have to do is simply lie there as well as allow your male permeate you. Yet you can be a little active if you want. You can place your arms behind you and scrub your man's legs. You can additionally flex your knees back so that your feet are delicately pressing your guy's butt and assisting him propelled into you. If you like, you can additionally elevate you butt slightly with each thrust for more difficult sex.

Male roles

Kissing in this position can injure your neck, however makes it a lot more intense!

Your man will certainly be doing the majority of the work in the Jockey position. He will certainly be thrusting in and also out. He will certainly likewise be able to alter his angle of access easily by leaning ahead or backwards as well as moving his whole body either forwards or backwards to make sure that he can strike many different areas inside you. The crucial to discovering a great angle is offering him some responses and letting him recognize what you are appreciating and also what you would certainly choose him to do.

In the Jockey position, your man is likewise in the ideal position to massage therapy your back as well as neck while he is upright or kiss you on your shoulders and also neck when his is leaning on top of you.

Tips

You can make use of the Jockey to excellent effect for both enchanting and slow-moving sex as well faster, more enthusiastic sex.

This is a fantastic position for rectal sex.

If you performing the Jockey infront of a wall surface or something strong, after that you can place your hands versus the wall and elevate your body somewhat so you can push back versus your guy with each drive.

The Jockey is an excellent position for people who such as to take control throughout sex or for ladies that like their male to be on top as well as in control.

Comments

I enjoy the Jockey position a lot. It's great for both slow-moving as well as faster, more passionate sex. It can really feel really intimate

7d. Rear Entry Sex Position

The Rear Entry sex position is fantastic for those that like their guys to be in control during sex, while also remaining quite intimate at the same time. The Rear Entry is very much like Spooning, however with the man on top.

You'll discover that the Rear Entry position creates some really intimate sex!

To do the Rear Entry, you first need to rest on your tummy on the bed with your legs open. Your male after that gets on top of you with his legs with each other in pretty much the very same position he would certainly be in while carrying out the Missionary position with you and then enters you. He then relaxes part of his weight on your back and part of it with his arms by placing his hands on the bed. In this manner you will feel him right on top of you without him squashing you as well as creating you taking a breath difficulties!

Woman roles

As the Rear Entry position is one with your male very much ahead, you can simply exist there as well as enjoy it. Yet you can likewise transform the angle your male permeates you at.

By planting your knees firmly on the bed, you'll find it fairly simple to lift your butt up into the air. Doing this will also assist you to thrust back right into your guy with each of his thrusts.

Guy roles

You man will certainly be doing the majority of the work in the Rear Entry. He can simply embeded and out using his hips. Or he can make use of more of a complete body movement to thrust backwards and forwards. Make sure to let him know what you favor him doing.

Your man will certainly likewise be on top of you. Some like really feeling the complete weight of the ir male push down on them, while others prefer to simply feel him a little press against them. Allow him understand what you like. Your man is likewise in a great position, when in addition to you like this to kiss you on your back as well as on the back of your neck contributing to the affection.

This position is perfect for transitioning to many of the Doggy style positions like the Bulldog or the Basset Hound.

Tips

Try varying how wide you hold your legs open, right from very open to truly close together to make it tighter for your person.

Try placing a cushion right under your waist/hips to elevate them as well as change the angle of entrance.

If you have a headboard or there is a wall in front of you, then you can place your hands on it and also press yourself back onto your man.

Remarks

I actually delight in the Rear Entry position. It feels both sensual as well as warm at the same time

7e. Superwoman Sex Position

The Superwoman position may sound like among those positions where you actually need to be like 'Superwoman' and do a great deal of work. Thankfully this is not the situation at all, your male will certainly be doing the majority of the work. In some ways the Superwoman is rather like the Life Raft position.

Executing the Superwoman position on a sofa can be a little awkward if it's not big sufficient, as you can see aware above.

To carry out the Superwoman, you need to relax on your bed on your tummy, with you arms resting on the bed, extended before you. While your stomach must get on the bed, your midsection will be at the side with your legs hanging over the side. Your guy will after that after that enter you while standing from behind as well as will certainly begin thrusting in and out.

Woman roles

When you are in the Superwoman position, you'll locate that it's difficult to do anything as you are relaxing on your belly and also your legs will either impend, being held by your man or gently touching the ground. You can use your arms to carefully push on your own back onto your man as he is penetrating you if you desire.

You can additionally attempt increasing your waistline slightly to alter the angle that your man is penetrating you at. To keep it raised, try putting a pillow under it.

Male roles

Your man will be doing the lions share of the operate in the Superwoman position. Clearly he is going to be embedding as well as out. He can do this by just utilizing his hips or he can make it even more of a full-body motion. To propelled with a little bit extra pressure, he can clinch your legs and lift them off the ground or he can grab you by placing his hands around your waistline.

He can additionally lean forward as well as rest his hands on your back or order your shoulders with them to pull you into him. He can also gently get your hair (or highly if you want).

Performing the Superwoman position on a table will certainly give you a lot more space.

Tips

The Superwoman is equally as good for those of you that take pleasure in anal sex as it is for those who like regular vaginal sex.

If your male grabs you by your legs, then he may harm your skin if he gets you too tough (it feels like he is stretching your skin). Make certain that he understands to be gentle with you.

Try experimenting with various angles from both you and also your guy, up until you discover something that feels ideal for both of you.

Comments

I directly take into consideration the Superwoman to be a 'middle-of-the-road' sex position. It's okay, yet does not feel fantastic. I feel that you ought to certainly try it out with your partner, yet do not other than it to be as mind blowing as various other positions.

Chapter 8. Dog Style Sex Positions

If you delight in 'taking it from behind' then you'll like all these various variants of Doggy Style! Doggy style sex is possibly the most discussed sex position. Most couples locate Doggy style sex to be hot and also naughty, while some locate it a fantastic means to strike angles they would not otherwise hit. Yet Doggy style does not simply include one position. There are a lot of different variants. Bassett Hound Position, Bulldog Position, Corner Doggy Position, Doggy Style Position, Fire Hydrant Position, Frog Leap Position, Leapfrog Position, Rear Admiral Position, Stairway To Heaven Position, Final Furlong Position, Turtle Position

8a. Bassett Hound Sex Position

The Bassett Hound sex position is a variation of routine Doggy Style, or the Leap Frog, depending on which way you consider it. It's an actually enjoyable position if you like to be a little submissive, while your guy takes control.

Right here you can see the man doing the Basset Hound, with his knees together. He can spread them out to reduced himself towards the bed if he suches as.

To do the Bassett Hound with your man, you require to come down on all fours. This suggests getting onto your knees as well as hands. From here, you then need to lower yourself better towards the ground. To do this, spread your knees out and press your butt in reverse. This will certainly decrease your waist. Reduced on your own onto your elbow joints and spread them out to bring your chest closer to the ground. Your male will certainly after that enter you from behind while on his knees. He can also spread his knees to get reduced or he can remain relatively upright as well as enter you from a tilted position.

If you want to get on your own low onto the bed, you need to have a decent amount of adaptability to do this position with your male.

Girl roles

When you remain in the Bassett Hound position, you are mosting likely to be doing basically the very same points as you would when in the Doggy style position, which suggests you won't be doing a great deal. You can press on your own back onto your male for more difficult penetration. You can also decrease your hand(s) as well as begin masturbating yourself.

Guy roles

When you are doing the Bassett Hound with your guy, he will have great deal of adaptability to do various points. He can decrease his midsection to yours as well as permeate you, merely moving in and out. Or he can maintain his waist elevated by keeping his knees better with each other and penetrate you from above to boost your G-Spot extra.

He can additionally place his hands on your shoulders or midsection and pull you towards him for harder infiltration. Or he can use his hands to massage therapy your back while fucking you or perhaps get to around your waistline and also begin rubbing your clitoris.

In this image you can see the man performing a variation of the Basset Hound. He is crouching down as opposed to kneeling.

Tips

You can carry out rectal sex just as quickly in the Bassett Hound position as normal genital sex.

If you are performing rectal sex with your guy, then he can finger you at the same time as he penetrates you for extra pleasure.

The Bassett Hound allows for actually deep infiltration, so be careful if your man has a relatively lengthy penis.

To aid you turn, you can attempt placing a pillow or support right under your waist to raise it.

Comments

I find that the Basset Hound is a terrific position to transfer to from Doggy Style. You might even find it more pleasant than routine Doggy Style. The secret is getting your male to attempt several positions for permeating you by transforming the placements of his knees.

8b. Bulldog Sex Position

The Bulldog sex position is extremely similar in a great deal of means to normal Doggy Style. You will certainly see when you try it that the Bulldog position puts you in an also extra submissive position than during Doggy Style sex.

The Bulldog is a fun variant of regular Doggy style, but gives it feels tighter for your guy.

To carry out the Bulldog, you need to first get down on all fours, on your hands and knees. Next you require to bring both of your legs together. Your man then enters you from behind in a small bowing position. He puts his feet beyond your legs and he can put his hands on your waistline or your shoulders to stable himself.

Woman roles

You are going to be rather passive for the most part when you are in the Bulldog position. This means that you do not have to do anything. However if you like, you can push on your own back onto your male to make each thrust from your male feel extra effective. The tighter you maintain your legs together, the tighter you will feel for your guy.

If you are having anal sex with your man, then you can try opening your legs a bit and placing your pass on there to start masturbating or thumbing on your own, while he is propelling.

Man roles

Your guy will certainly be doing practically all of the effort when carrying out the Bulldog. He will be squatting right over your butt as well as embedding as well as out. But due to the position he remains in, he can very easily transform his angle of entry. This is can function actually well if you provide him comments so he can locate something that you both actually appreciate.

If you want a lot more passionate or perhaps rougher sex with your man, after that he can clinch your hips, your shoulders or even your hair and also draw you right into him as he is propelling. Doing this is likewise terrific for when you like your man being more dominant, while you take on an extra submissive role. While making love in this position, you can rest on your shoulders and upper body if you locate that your hands are burning out. This transforms the Bulldog right into something much more like the Leapfrog position.

Attempt performing the Bulldog in front of a wall as well as use your hands to press back versus your male if you such as more extreme sex.

Tips

- This is a terrific position for your man to really feel actually leading in, however ensure that he doesn't obtain as well carried away by fucking you too passionately or as well hard.

- It does not always have to be a dominant/submissive position. Your man can thrust really carefully as well as massage therapy your back with his hands at the same time if you desire it to be extra intimate.

- Make certain to maintain great interaction with your partner to allow him recognize what you are appreciating and what he can do better (e.g. lean forwards/backwards, thrust faster/slower, etc).

8c. Corner Doggy Style Sex Position.

The Corner Doggy Style sex position is a truly excellent variation of regular Doggy Style sex. While it is carried out on the edge of your bed or table, just like the likewise called Corner Cowgirl, it has really little else in common with it.

You can carry out the Corner Doggy position on a bed or on a table like aware over.

To perform Corner Doggy Style, you need to start by standing upright on the flooring with one leg positioned on either side of the corner of your bed/table. You then need to lean over onto the bed/table hing on either your arm joints or hands. Your guy then permeates you from behind, like he would certainly throughout Doggy Style or the Bodyguard.

Woman roles.

When in the Corner Doggy Style position, you have a lot of options and also variations that you can do. You can remain in position with your hands and arm joints on the bed/table as well as gently push back right into your man.

Alternatively you can instead bring your body reduced, by flexing your knees so that you are resting on your stomach as opposed to sustaining yourself with your hands/elbows). Since you go to the edge of the bed/table, you will certainly find that you can quickly spread your legs very wide without it becoming also awkward.

Guy roles.

Your guy has several alternatives in the Corner Doggy Style position. He can solve over you to offer you a feeling that he truly controlling you. To do this he needs to make certain your legs are spread and he is fairly upright and also leaning right over you.

He can hold onto your hips as well as pull you in with each drive if you both desire even more passionate sex. Additionally, he can get your shoulders and even your hair (simply make sure that he does not draw too tough!). A really great thing that your man can do in the Corner Doggy Style postion if he wishes to make the sex a lot more sensuous and also charming is to carefully massage as well as massage your back while thrusting. This position is excellent for when your guy intends to reach about as well as begin masturbating you or even finger you.

Tips.

This is an excellent position for enthusiastic, even rough sex with your man. Your man can propelled quite hard without you going anywhere due to the fact that you're wedged into the corner of the bed/table.

By you flexing your knees and also changing your height, together with your man readjusting his elevation, you can accomplish many different angles of access when carrying out Corner Doggy Style, which suggests that you will certainly generally discover a 'place' that you really delight in.

The Corner Doggy Style position is ideal for both anal and genital sex.

You cannot execute the Corner Doggy Style position on a bed that has both a headboard as well as footboard.

Comments.

I really do delight in the Corner Doggy Style sex position. It's truly versatile, making it ideal for both slow, sensuous sex as well as even more extensive, animalistic sex as well as every little thing in between. If you discover that you are getting bored with normal Doggy Style, I very suggest that you attempt it.

8d. Dog Style Sex Position

There are a big number of variants to the classic Doggy Style sex position (like the Stairway To Heaven Position), which is excellent for both anal and genital sex with your companion.

Doggy style is just one of one of the most popular sex positions. The good news is it doesn't call for a lots of adaptability to perform.

To perform Doggy Style with your male, you require to first come down on your hands as well as knees with your legs spread a little apart. Your male obtains down on his knees as well as enters you from behind (facing your back) while on his knees in an upright position. He can after that grab your midsection with his hands or put them on your back or grab your shoulders.

Woman roles.

When you remain in the Doggy Style position, you do not need to do much. If you desire more challenging infiltration, then you can push back onto your male with each stroke. Or you can make use of one hand to masturbate throughout it. You can change the angle he is permeating you at by moving your head and also shoulders closer to the ground.

Man roles.

When you are in the Doggy style position, your guy will simply be propelling in and also out. He can transform the angle of entry if he leans back or forwards a little. When your male lags you, he is in the perfect position to reach around as well as begin rubbing your clit and even thumbing your if you are having anal sex.

For extra power, your guy can keep your midsection or your shoulders. If you like it rough, after that he can get your hair as well as pull on it.

Just make sure to inform him how difficult you like it!

During Doggy style, your man can place his hands on your waistline or grab your shoulders, or if you like it a little rougher, he can order your hair.

Tips.

If you discover that your arms are obtaining tired from remaining in this position, then try doing it on the flooring beside a bed or a couch so that you can relax your head, shoulders and upper body on it and take the weight off your hands.

Another alternate variant is standing Doggy Style. When you are carrying out standing doggy design, you will certainly need to maintain your legs fairly straight and also have your hands on a relatively safe as well as stable things like a table, chair or bed.

A great deal of people do not locate Doggy Style to be that intimate. It's even more of a warm, sometimes dirty and sexy position like the Betty Rocker position.

If you are follower of your man being extremely dominant as well as taking control, after that you'll like Doggy Style as your man can grab you from behind as well as actually fuck you set.

Comments.

I truly appreciate Doggy Style. It certainly isn't one of the most intimate position you'll ever make love in, yet it can be really warm.

8e. Fire Hydrant Sex Position.

The Fire Hydrant sex position is a variation of routine Doggy Style that some pairs love while others are not so crazy about it. To execute it just needs a little of additional adaptability.

To establish it up, you both require to enter the routine Doggy Style position. This means that you need to come down on your hands as well as knees, dealing with in the direction of the floor. Your male will certainly then get on his knees behind you. He requires to have his knees inside your own. Your man is after that going to begin raising one of his legs upwards as well as forwards and also plant his foot on the flooring to your side. In doing so he will raise your leg on that side, to make sure that your upper leg will currently be resting on top his thigh. This will certainly make you resemble a canine peeing on a fire hydrant.

The Fire Hydrant can be a fun variation of the routine Doggy style position.

Lady roles.
Initially you may find the Fire Hydrant position to be fairly uncomfortable. Your leg that is resting on your guy's upper leg might feel a little bit weird, however if you want (and are versatile sufficient) you can cover it around your man's waist/leg and draw on your own better right into him.

Besides that, you will certainly be doing whatever you have usually been carrying out in the normal Doggy Style position. This means you will be pushing yourself into your man. You can also experiment by hing on either your hands or elbows to find which is most comfortable.

Guy roles.
Since the Fire Hydrant position can be potentially fairly unpleasant as well as little unpleasant for you, your guy's initial concern is ensuring that you are comfortable. He can help to adjust how you rest your leg on his thigh. He can then start thrusting into you once you are comfortable.

If he leans over you like he can throughout Doggy Style, after that he is going to place extra stress on your increased leg if you are not that versatile, so he requires to remain upright and even lean back a bit. He can nevertheless grab your by the waistline, shoulders or hair.

Tips.
Some girls simply discover it to be not enjoyable and uncomfortable in any way. So do not fret if you don't like it. Lots of girls don't specifically enjoy it.

Anal sex is somewhat more difficult than vaginal sex in the Fire Hydrant position. This is because your guy is increasing you upwards, which elevates your rectum even more away from his penis.

Some women discovered that their raised leg constrained up in this position.

Remarks.

For me directly, I locate the Fire Hydrant position to feel almost the like normal Doggy Style.

8f. Frog Leap Sex Position.

The Frog Leap position is typically perplexed with the Leapfrog position as a result of their comparable names. Both positions involve your man penetrating you from behind, they are quite different.

To enter into the Frog Leap position, you require to begin by squatting down by flexing your knees and leaning forward to ensure that your hands get on the flooring in front of you, keeping you balanced. This is why it's called the Frog Leap; you will look quite like a frog about to make a jump. Your man after that gets behind you on his knees as well as enters you as he would certainly if you were having normal Doggy Style sex with him.

You may discover performing the Frog Leap position to be a little hard without something to keep to stable on your own. Try doing next to a wall/chair.

Girl roles.

The most integral part of the Frog Leap position is entering the bowing position at the ideal elevation to make sure that your guy can enter you and offer deep sufficient penetration without it feeling also uncomfortable for you. You can achieve this by adjusting just how much you spread your legs apart as well as where you position your hands (before you/to your side/directly listed below you).

Afterwards, it's just a situation of leaning back towards your guy. Or if you want to offer him a remainder after that you can returned into him. If you don't feel like propelling, then you can relocate your hips backwards and forwards on his penis.

If you find the Frog Leap position uncomfortable, after that attempt doing it before a bed so that you can rest part of your weight on the bed rather than using your hands.

Guy roles.

Your guy is going to be doing everything he requires to do throughout routine Doggy Style sex. This means that he needs to thrust in and out using his hips. To help him do this, he should grab onto your waist or lean forward and order your shoulders. If you want something a little more kinky, then he can grab hold of your hair.

He can put a cushion or 2 under them if he his not high enough on his knees.

Tips.

The Frog Leap is best for both rectal as well as vaginal sex.

- A wonderful variant of the Frog Leap is for your male to be on his feet, flexing his knees slightly while standing right over you to make sure that he can permeate you from above. This is a terrific position if you like to really feel dominated by your guy.

- Your guy remains in the perfect position to get to about and start scrubing your clit if you such as. If you are having anal sex, he can even start fingering you.

Comments.

I such as the Frog Leap position. It's a great modification from normal Doggy and also it's easy to change to, although if you don't have a little degree of adaptability, then you might find that it obtains tiring truly rapidly.

8g. Leapfrog Sex Position.

The leapfrog position is extremely, very comparable to normal doggy style. To execute the leapfrog, you simply need to think the routine Doggy style position, which suggests that the man is upright while on his knees, behind you. You after that also need to jump on your knees. Yet instead of getting on your elbow joints, like you would certainly be when executing doggy style, you require to rest your breast as well as directly the bed much like in the picture below, while protruding your bottom in the air, to ensure that your man can conveniently enter you. Your male will certainly have his legs close together inside yours.

The Leapfrog is terrific for changing the angle you receive your male at when compared to regular Doggy style.
Your male can place his hands on your back while he is embedding and also out, or additionally he can order your hips so that he can thrust with even more force for even more strenuous sex. It's really as much as you how high you want to increase your bottom. You can have it rather low and also placed pillows or paddings under your lower belly/waist to give assistance. Or you can elevate it up fairly high. You can also get onto your feet and think a crouching position like you would if you were playing the game leap frog. If you do enter a crouching position, then your guy will need to reach his feet also.

Lady roles.
When you are in the jump frog position, your man will certainly be doing most of the job. He will be embedding as well as out. You can also thrust versus your man for even more vigorous sex, however additionally to give him a rest if he is burning out.
In this position, it's very simple to start promoting your clit as well as masturbating while your man is embedding as well as out, which will just include in the experience. You can also reach back and start massaging your man's testicles while he is fucking you if your arms are long enough. By leaning forwards or backwards, you can increase or lower your hips, which will create various angles of entry. You can also stand up onto your feet and also get involved in a squatting position to change it up (although you will discover this position gets tiring very promptly!).

Guy roles.
Your guy will get on his knees, behind you with his legs inside yours. Entering you is really simple in this position. His basic technique is just embedding and also out. By leaning backwards, away from you or forwards and over you, he can change his angle of entry, meaning that he can change which spot he is stimulating and rubbing.
Your man is likewise in a terrific postion where he can provide some hands-on excitement with his hands. He can reach over and under you to begin massaging your clitoris.

Executing the Leapfrog versus a wall surface (or head board) is great as it permits you to push back versus your guy.

Tips.

By carrying out the leap frog before a wall and also positioning your hands on it means that you can push back against your guy to ensure that his thrusting feels a whole lot stronger.

This position permits really deep penetration, which can be unpleasant for some.

You can make it tighter for your male by keeping your legs together rather than apart.

Remarks.

The leapfrog is a truly terrific position for nearly all pairs due to the fact that you don't have to be adaptable or solid to do it. You also can quickly maneuver a lot in the leapfrog up until your male is striking an actually good spot.

8h. Back Admiral Sex Position.

The Rear Admiral sex position is fantastic for those that like be controlled by their guy and for him to be in nearly complete control. You can carry out the Rear Admiral while standing up or while on your knees.

Standing

To execute it while standing, both you and also your male need to be encountering parallel while both standing. Your guy requires to after that enter you from behind, either vaginally or anally. You after that require to flex over so that you tolerate is parallel to the ground and also you are encountering the floor. You can spread your legs while your man keeps his close together or vice-versa. You put your arms parallel with your body. You man then keeps your hands/wrists as well as begins thrusting in as well as out.

You'll like the Rear Admiral position if you like your man being leading in bed.
In this position, your male can thrust in and also out quite deep and really hard too if that's what you both appreciate.

On Your Knees
When executing the Rear Admiral on your knees, you do whatever as you would when you were standing, except both you and also your guy will certainly be on your knees. You need to spread your knees vast and also your male can keep his close together or vice/versa. If you such as, you can additionally lean down a little and also rest your head as well as shoulders on the bed.
This is why it's called the Rear Admiral. Your man is in control of the 'ship' (you).

Girl roles
Your man will certainly be doing many of the job when you are in the Rear Admiral position. You do need to offer him directions from time to time, so that he understands how fast and also just how deep you like it. It's likewise crucial to let him understand if he is drawing as well difficult on your arms. Besides this, you will have very little control.

Man roles
When your man is in the Rear Admiral position, he will have nearly total control, which is a major turn on for a great deal of girls. He can lean backwards or forwards to transform the angle of entry. He can additionally stop propelling and rather grind up against you in a round or figure of 8 movement.
If your guy can utilize 1 just one of his hands to hold both your hands, after that he can utilize his freedom to start rubbing your clitoris. Or if you are having anal sex with him, he can finger you.

Tips
If it's your first time trying it, see to it to tell your man what you like and also how difficult to fuck you. Otherwise he might get carried away and mistakenly injure you.
.This position is ideal for those of you that like anal sex with your male remains in an extremely dominant position.

.Make certain to explore this position while on your knees in addition to while standing to see which you prefer.

Back Admiral Variation

There is a variation of the Rear Admiral that is a 'funny' or joke sex position. To execute it, you do it similar to you would certainly when standing, except your man is not holding your arms as well as you are not holding on to him. Rationale is that he requires to you to attempt and also stay well balanced as well as maintain his penis inside you as he moves you onward around the space with each thrust. When your total a complete lap of the area, you have finished the Rear Admiral! Doing this is a truly fun modification from the routine Rear Admiral.

8i. Stairway To Heaven Sex Position

The Stairway To Heaven sex position is really simply a variant of regular Doggy Style. The truly good thing about it is that you are performing it with your man on stairs.

Prior to you do anything, I would initially recommend you to experiment with the Stairway To Heaven position on a staircases that is covered in rug. If you do it on a difficult stairways you might discover it sore on your joints and also knees.

You require to establish yourself up to make sure that your knees get on a lower step as well as you hands get on a greater action. It's truly up to you how much you intend to extend on your own out. Your male then enters you from behind. He might find it a bit challenging to get his elevation right. If he stands on the action below your knees after that he may still be above you. He can simply bend his knees to reduced himself down to you or you can elevate or lower your hips if so.

Lady roles

You are going to be rather easy with your man taking a much extra active role when you are in the Stairway To Heaven position. If you choose, you can simply hold on your own in position while your guy drives right into you. If you desire harder, a lot more forceful drives after that you can place your hands on the stairways and push back against him.

You can likewise get to down with one hand and start masturbating on your own while he is fucking you. You can begin fingering on your own if you are having anal sex.

Guy roles

Your man is just mosting likely to be embedding as well as out utilizing his hips mostly. If he wants to penetrate you harder and also deeper, after that he can clinch your waist with a hand on either side of it or he can order your shoulders or even your hair.

Your guy is also in a truly great position to reach around and also start rubbing your clitoris when in the Stairway To Heaven position while penetrating you at the same time.

Tips

If the rug is harsh) or there is no rug at all, - It can harm your knees and also arm joints. Take care

- The Stairway To Heaven is ideal for both anal and vaginal sex.

When you cannot wait to get to the room with your male, - This position is ideal for!

Comments

I highly recommend the Stairway To Heaven position. It's truly fantastic to try it as it takes you out of the room as well as produces a remarkable adjustment. Selection is the seasoning of life.

8j. Last Furlong Sex Position

The Final Furlong is a truly good variant of Doggy Style. It's simple to execute as well as does not take much initiative. It's also far more intimate than Doggy Style. The Final Furlong gets it's name from the fact that you both resemble you are riding a horse like a jockey.The hardest feature of carrying out the Final Furlong with your guy is locating the ideal furniture! Due to the fact that you will both be sitting in the same position, this is. Ideally you will certainly have a foot rest or vast feces that can accommodate both of you. You both need to take a seat, straddling the stool/foot remainder while dealing with the same instructions. Your male will lag you. You need to lean over somewhat so he can conveniently enter you. Then as soon as he is inside you, he can hold you close like you are in the Spoons position and start thrusting.

Lady roles

The Final Furlong position does not require excessive effort that makes it great for sluggish, sensuous sex. To boost the affection, you can lean backwards in the direction of your man and also place your arms carefully around his head or back. If it's comfortable to do so, you can push back against your male for more challenging penetration. Other than that, you should simply kick back and also take pleasure in the flight.

Guy roles

Your man will certainly be doing a little bit extra in the Final Furlong position. He will certainly be thrusting in and out. If he elevates himself off the stool/footrest a little, he'll discover it easier to thrust in an out. To assist with embedding and out, he must place his arms around you: either around your waistline or under your arms and after that getting your shoulders. He can likewise reach around as well as hold your busts.

The Final Furlong is a just as great position for both anal and also vaginal sex.

Tips

- Even though it has a name that recommends it takes a lot of effort, the Final Furlong is an actually remarkable position if you wish to have sensual as well as slow-moving sex with your man without needing to be very versatile or strong.

- It makes for an actually great mix when your guy switches from embedding an out, to grinding his hips and making a figure of 8 activity inside of you.

- The Final Furlong is a beautiful position if you like using a vibrator during sex.

Remarks

I am a large follower of the Final Furlong as it really feels good for relaxed, easy sex in addition to even more sensual sex. Your guy can likewise order your hair in this position.

8k. Turtle Sex Position

The Turtle position is a nice variation of Doggy Style where your man is significantly in a leading position.

The Turtle sex position is a kind of Doggy Style sex that needs a little bit of versatility. When you are starting to obtain bored of routine Doggy Style, it's an easy way to flavor things up with your man.

To get into the Turtle position, you first need to be residing your knees on the flooring. When in this position, reduced yourself down so that your bottom is sitting on top of the back's of your ankles. Following lean as far ahead as you can. You can grab hold of your legs before you to aid lean better ahead. Your male will be on his knees behind you permeating you. He may discover that he needs to readjust his elevation to make it less complicated for himself by either spreading his knees or bringing them together.

Lady roles

You'll locate that you can barely move when you are in the in the Turtle position. If you like your male taking control throughout sex while you continue to be relatively non-active, this is excellent. But if you like, you can gently push back versus your guy. Something you do have a great deal of control over is the angle of infiltration. You can regulate it by elevating as well as lowering your upper body until you find something that you really enjoy.

Guy roles

Your man will certainly be doing similar activity he does when in any type of Doggy position, such as the Bassett Hound position. He simply requires to embeded as well as out (forwards as well as in reverse). To aid himself do this, he can place his hands on your waist/hips and carefully hold onto to. If he desires he can additionally lean over you and keep your shoulders. For a little more kinky sex, he can hold you by your hair (simply ensure that he does not harm you!).

Tips

- Don't fail to remember to attempt differing the angle of access up until you find what's most enjoyable.

- If your male desires, he can actually stand on his feet and crouch over you rather than resting on his knees.

- As with all Doggy Style positions, the Turtle is wonderful for anal sex.

If you have negative knees then you may desire to avoid this position, -.

Remarks

The Turtle is rather very easy for both partners to do, which makes for a nice change for when you find yourselves obtaining burnt out of Doggy style or something similar. One point I have actually discovered though is that when you remain in the Turtle position you will be encountering the flooring which for one reason or another I find to be less intimate than a lot of the other 'from behind' placements.

chapter 9. Kneeling Sex Positions

Occasionally it's truly enjoyable to switch things up and also to try having sex while stooping. When many folks first start trying out brand-new sex positions, they immediately try variants of one of the most usual positions, like Missionary or Doggy style. It turns out that the majority of these 'regular' positions involve you either lying on your back or on your belly. For a great deal of pairs, these variations of 'routine' placements are simply too comparable. Why not attempt out some of the kneeling positions below if you are finding this to be the case. They all entail you getting on your knees. Flexed Knee Position, Book Ends Position, Dublin Shuffle Position, Shoe Shiner Position, Tea spooning Position

9a. Flexed Knee Sex Position

The Bended Knee sex position is one the you possibly never even assumed of, which is a good idea. Why? Which is the perfect means to show him that you are adventurous in the room because it means that you can surprise your guy with it. Some people see the Bended Knee as a less complicated version of the Ballerina.

Lots of people have never ever also thought about the flexed knee, that makes it's an enjoyable change in the bedroom!

To perform the Bended Knee position, both get on your knees while encountering each other in an upright position. Make certain you are actually close to each other. Your guy then needs to stay on one knee, while lifting his other knee up and also growing his foot on the bed to his side. You after that need to lift your leg on the exact same side and also rest it on top of his. Your guy after that enters you as well as starts propelling. You'll find that you need a bit of flexibility and also stamina to execute it for long periods.

You will certainly be able to maintain your balance better by welcoming each other.

Lady roles

When you are doing the Bended Knee with your man, you don't have a great deal to do other than thrusting back onto your male. You need to keep your man by covering your arms around his midsection or by placing them underneath his arms and ordering his shoulders.

You can utilize your leg resting on top of your male's legs as a sort of lever, assisting to press on your own up and down. But don't fret excessive about that. You must invest even more time concentrating on embracing your guy and also kissing him passionately on the lips, face and neck.

If you are flexible, you can wrap your leg around his to 'hold' him to make sure that you can pull yourself right into him.

Guy roles

Your guy is misting likely to be both pulling you in towards him in a welcome and propelling into you also. He can put his hands under your butt and also lift assistance to lift you up. While propelling, he can hold you close and kiss you on the lips and also neck or run his hands via your hair.

Tips

It does not truly offer that much pleasure from penetration, unless you enjoy shallow penetration. A couple of have actually explained it as little bit more than a stretching workout!

You can accomplish much deeper infiltration if you tilt on your own to the side.

Although people have found the sex to be so-so when in the Bended Knee position, they still located it to be quite intimate as well as 'close'. This is specifically real when you embrace your man snugly.

Remarks

The Bended Knee knee is a position that does not permit very deep penetration, which is good if your man has a lengthy penis or you like to have the initial few inches of you vagina stimulated as opposed to all of it

9b. Book Ends Sex Position

Guide Ends position is a pretty intriguing one. For a great deal of pairs doing it, they will really locate it very hard to achieve infiltration easily. That's not to say that it's not a fun love making position though!

Supplied you as well as your male have fairly comparable elevations, guide Ends position can be really intimate.

To perform guide Ends position, you as well as your male need to both get on your knees dealing with each other on your bed. Your male needs to spread out his knees to ensure that he can reduce himself while you will require to remain as tall as possible. When your man is then a little listed below you, he can slip his penis inside (you might require to assist lead it in). He can after that bring his legs with each other again and begin to raise himself upwards if it's comfy. You can also lean in reverse to make infiltration deeper and also extra pleasurable for your male.

You most likely will not be able to do actual penetrative sex in the Book Ends position if your man is a lot taller than you

Girl roles

When in guide Ends position you may discover that long, deep strokes are just not feasible. An option is to just grind on your male instead by turning your hips while he's inside you.

This is the excellent position for you to pull
your male in close and kiss him!

For many pairs, the Book Ends position is much more concerning affection than sex, so you might locate that it's finest to invest even more time focusing on obtaining close to him, kissing him and embracing him. Make sure to cover your arms around your man and to kiss him on his lips, cheek, neck as well as ears. You can additionally make it a little bit more sexy by running your fingers with his hair and carefully damaging his scalp.

Man roles

Initially he may locate that he elopes a fair bit if he is pursuing longer strokes which he might be better off simply grinding up against you. He can wrap his arms around your midsection as well as butt to bring you closer to him.

He requires to focus on enhancing intimacy in this position. So this implies that generally, your male will be doing basically the exact same things as you. This indicates he requires to get near to you, hold you, kiss you as well as rub your back and head with his hands and also arms.

Tips

Sometimes there is no demand for penetration. Rather your guy must simply try using his prick to rub the beyond your vagina instead of thrusting inside it.

In this position you are inches from your male's face. This makes it ideal for making deep eye contact with him. Great for bonding!

If you take pleasure in really feeling close as well as covered by your guy, then you'll such as doing the Book Ends with him.

Comments

I discover that guide Ends position is ideal for sexual activity, especially best before you make love. It's additionally great for feeling closer to your man and also for showing him that you truly like him. It's additionally helpful for transitioning to giving him a blowjob or for him to go down on you as well as consume you out.

9c. Dublin Shuffle Sex Position

The Dublin Shuffle sex position is an enjoyable one and is excellent for pairs who such as the intimacy of dealing with each other during sex together with the enjoyable of both being upright throughout it. The factor that it's called the Dublin Shuffle is since there is commonly a lot of evasion involved to find the precise right angle or 'area'. To get into position for the Dublin Shuffle, your man requires to start by basing on the flooring, while you stoop on the bed. You will certainly be encountering each other. Before you go any type of better, you need to see to it that the base of his penis goes to regarding the same height as your vaginal area. Otherwise, then put a few sturdy publications under the bed to elevate it, or obtain your guy to depend on something to make sure that you are both at the ideal height. When you are both at a good elevation, your man can then enter you.

Girl roles
When in the Dublin Shuffle with your guy, you won't obtain a massive amount of enjoyment if you simply stay upright the whole time. You'll locate it far more rewarding to lean backwards. How far you lean back depends on you.

Your male can assist support you as well as you can put your hands around his waistline if you lean back just a little bit. Attempt putting your hands behind you on the bed if you want to lean back additionally. If you are leaning back as well as he is holding your or you are using one hand to support on your own, you will certainly be conveniently able to rub your clit with your free hand. For a great deal of men, seeing you massage your clitoris as well as masturbate on your own in front of the m is a major turn on.

Guy roles
Your male has really little to do in the Dublin Shuffle. At least, he just requires to get involved in position and also embed and out. Yet if he intends to do even more, then he can aid support you. If you are upright in the Dublin Shuffle, then your guy will certainly be in the excellent position to kiss you and hold you close. If you are leaning back, then he can place his hands on your breasts and also carefully scrub them.

Tips
- Most importantly, make sure to mess around in the Dublin Shuffle position in the beginning until you locate an angle that you really appreciate. You may discover that you enjoy it finest when you lean thus far back that you are practically lying down on your back.

- If the bed or your male is not quite at the best elevation, attempt spreading your legs to reduced on your own or your male can hop on his toes to increase himself greater.

9d. Shoe Shiner Sex Position

The Shoe Shiner has a little bit in common with the Bended Knee position as you are both encountering each other while on just one knee. It additionally among those positions that you've probably never tried previously.

To set it up, both you and your male are mosting likely to be facing each other on your knees. You ought to be so close that you are hugging each other. You are then mosting likely to both elevate your left knees so that your upper legs are alongside the bed and also your reduced legs are vertical with your left feet firmly on the bed. This will certainly allow your guy to easily enter you.

The majority of people have never also taken into consideration something like the shoe black eye. This makes it fantastic to attempt if you find yourself obtaining tired with the 'normal' sex positions.

If he is much taller in this position, then you require to place a pillow/cushion under your knee to increase you high enough.

Girl roles

When you first enter the Shoe Shiner position, you might discover it to be a little uncomfortable. You won't be able to have especially fast sex or lengthy strokes.

But the distance will certainly offset this. The Shoe Shiner is even more of an intimate position for you and also your man. You can push on your own onto your guy with each brief stroke or push back against him while he is grinding on you. You should cover your arms around his waist as well as back or place them under his arms as well as hold onto his shoulders. You can also kiss him on his neck, cheeks, lips and ears. You can additionally put your hands on his butt to draw him right into you with each stroke.

As you can see, the Shoe Shiner is extremely comparable to the Bended Knee.

Guy roles

When doing the Shoe Shiner, your man just needs to get right into a wonderful constant rhythm. He'll discover that he can't take lengthy strokes as a result of the position that he's in, but instead needs to make much shorter ones.

Your man can likewise place his arms around you. He'll locate that he's in the perfect position to run his fingers through your scalp or perhaps lightly pull on your hair. He can also put his hands on your butt also and also draw you in with each stroke. He can additionally maintain you constantly drew versus him, while he grinds on your clit with his pubic bone.

Tips

- The Shoe Shiner is fantastic for when you wish to try something various while having slow-moving, passionate sex.

- You will certainly locate having rectal sex in the Shoe Shiner position to be actually hard.
- If you are flexible, after that try leaning either forwards or in reverse with your man to transform the angle of infiltration.
- Don't neglect to switch knees if you find it getting unpleasant.

9e. Tea spooning Sex Position

As is really evident from the name, Tea spooning is a variation of normal Spooning.

Tea spooning with your man creates some actually intimate sex. It's likewise really simple to transition to this position from most Doggy Style positions.

To Teaspoon with your guy (or carry out the Tea spooning position), your guy needs to get onto his knees on either the bed or the flooring. He then requires to open his knees fairly vast. You after that require to get on your knees also while facing in the same direction as your man before him.

You need to have your knees with each other so that your man can turn up close behind you and enter you. When he does, he should cover his arms around you. He can place them around your waistline or on your breasts or under your arms to hold onto your shoulders. Entering into the Tea spooning position from regular Doggy Style sex is truly simple.

Lady roles

When in the Tea spooning position with your man, you have the option of letting him take control and doing all the propelling and also grinding. But if you like, you can bounce backwards and forwards on your knees and do a lot of the propelling also.

You can also place your arms backwards around your guy's waist or perhaps back as well as around his neck while he is kissing you. For affection, you need to attempt leaning right back versus your male so that you can really feel as much of his body on you as possible.

Male roles

When in the Tea spooning position with your man, he simply requires to carefully thrust in as well as out. Keep in mind, it's delicately, not hard. The Tea spooning position is about affection, which suggests that hard, strenuous propelling will wreck the ambience.

To contribute to the affection, your man ought to likewise be kissing you on the neck, cheeks and also shoulders. He is additionally in the excellent position to run his hands and also fingers up the back of your scalp (it feels remarkable). As he is so close to you, he can drop his hand towards your groin and carefully begin to massage you clit while permeating you at the same time or if you are having anal sex, then he can finger you.

Tips

Tea spooning is actually intimate. So you might discover that utilizing it the first time you make love with your guy, may make it appear like you are 'beginning a little solid'. It's finest to utilize after you have actually had sex with your male a few times.

It's incredibly very easy to change to something like Doggy Style or the Bassett Hound from Teaspooning.

Comments

I very suggest Tea spooning to everybody. I discover that it's practically better than routine spooning with your companion. It's also ideal for in front of a mirror to ensure that both of you can see whatever.

Chapter10. Resting on Your Man's Lap Sex Positions

Sex positions, where you take a seat your mans lap can make for some truly intimate sex. Any type of sex position where you are muffling your male's lap means that you can make a lot of body contact with him. When you want to have even more intimate sex, Perfect for!: After Dinner Position, Back Seat Driver Position, Bouncing Spoon Position, Lap Dance Position, Lotus Position, Mastery Position, See Saw Position, Side Ride Position, Side Saddle Position, Sofa Surprise Position

10a. After Dinner Sex Position

The After Dinner sex position is kind of comparable to the Back Seat Driver position. As you can most likely imagine, the name for the After Dinner sex position originates from the fact that you make use of a table as well as chair to do it, making it best for right after a dish!

As you can see from the picture, the After Dinner position is excellent for ... after dinner!

To carry out the After Dinner position, your guy needs to muffle a chair that is 2 feet from a table facing it, with his legs open fairly large. You after that need to back yourself up into your man with your legs rather close together in a standing position. Optionally, your male can then raise his legs up from the ground as well as put them on the table. When he does this, you will certainly be 'entraped' between his legs.

Girl roles

When you are in the After Dinner position, your legs will be together and also somewhat bent as well as you will be 'bouncing' backwards and forwards on your man's shaft. You can place your hands on the table before you to steady yourself as well as control exactly how quick you move up and down. You can also just sit down on his lap with his penis inside and also just gyrate your hips as well as rub yourself on him.

Alternatively, you can place your hands on your guy's legs to help press yourself upwards as well as downwards. If you do place your hands on his legs, then try to put them on his thighs, near to his hips as this will put extremely little stress on him. Stay clear of placing your hands on his shins or knees as you may harm him.

Male roles

Your male will certainly be resting on the chair, with his back leaning up against the back of the chair when executing the After Dinner with you. But he still will be doing several of the work. He can place his hands on your waist as well as help to lift you backwards and forwards on him. Or he can place them on your shoulders and also draw you down with each stroke for a lot more effective sex.

He is likewise in an excellent position when doing the After Dinner to massage your breasts or masturbate you or perhaps finger you if you are having anal sex.

Attempt trying out your legs far apart and then with them close together like in this image.

Tips

The After Dinner position is terrific for anal sex in addition to vaginal. When you are in this position, it's very easy to carry out both

You might not originally enjoy the After Dinner that a lot. My advice is to attempt it out a great couple of times prior to offering up on it. You may locate that you appreciate it a lot even more by leaning forwards or in reverse to locate an actually great place.

When you are executing the After Dinner, your guy is in the excellent position to massage therapy your back and also neck in addition to kiss them too.

Remarks

The best way to establish the After Dinner up is to stun your guy with it after cooking him his favored dish. If you are putting on a short outfit as well as no panties, after that you can swiftly enter into this position without much problem, which will certainly end up making the whole thing a great deal hotter!

10b. The Back Seat Driver Sex Position

The Back Seat Driver sex position is fantastic for pairs that obtain bored of only making love while one or both of the m is resting on the bed.

When you are having sex in the Back Seat Driver position, your male will be resting on a the edge of a chair or a sofa or even the bed with his legs spread broad as well as his feet on the floor. You after that require to support onto your male's crotch and also allow him gradually move his penis inside you while bending your knees.

When he is easily inside you, utilize your legs to bounce up and down him. Both you and your guy will certainly be encountering in the same direction for the Back Seat Driver.

The Back Seat Driver is a small variant on the Lap Dance position.

Girl roles

When you are in the Back Seat Driver lovemaking position, you will certainly be doing a lot of the work, jumping up and down on your male. If you are not utilized to this position or otherwise that fit, then you might find that you're legs start to burn out fairly quickly. By leaning forwards or backwards, you can change the angle that your guy is permeating you at.

You can put your hands on your male's upper legs and also use your arms to help push on your own up with each stroke if your legs are beginning to get tired from doing all the job.

Male roles

Your guy can do literally no work at done in the Back Seat Driver position. He can nearly remain still, however that's no fun. For faster and much more effective infiltration, he can put his hands around your hips and draw you down with each stroke. Or you can lean forwards and your male can place his arms over your back as well as grab hold of your shoulders and also pull you in towards him with each stroke. If your male is strong enough, he can put his hands under your bum and also provide your some assistance training you up and down.

He can additionally place his hands around your waist as well as can massage your clitoris. If you are having anal sex in the Back Seat Driver position, after that your man can finger you while you are jumping up and down on his penis.

Tips

- As I have currently stated, you can get tired extremely promptly if you are not extremely in shape or have not attempted the Back Seat Driver prior to.

- For those that such as rectal sex, this is a fantastic position, because both you and your man can still easily promote your vaginal area and also clit.

- In this position, you are the one in control, so if that's something that you don't such as, then you may not enjoy this position that a lot

When existing down or in bed, - The Back Seat Driver position is a wonderful change for pairs that generally just have sex. You can make use of the Back Seat Driver practically throughout your house, in the bed room, living space, kitchen area, etc.

Comments Below's something that I extremely recommend that you try with your guy at some point, he will certainly love it: The Back Seat Driver is best if you desire to make a sex session all concerning him. You can begin by sitting him down on a chair and afterwards doing a striptease for him. When you are finished offering him an erotic dance, you can then begin to give him a blowjob for a couple of minutes before having sex in the Back Seat Driver position with him. You could even take it a little more and tie him to the chair first!

10c. Bouncing Spoon Sex Position

The Bouncing Spoon sex position is a type of pseudo-spooning position for you and your male. It's a fairly easy position to do which makes it wonderful for spicing points up in the bedroom.

To execute it, your man needs to sit upright in bed with his back to the wall as well as his legs with each other and relatively straight (they do not have to be completely straight). You after that need to stand right over him with your back to him. Your feet should get on either side of this thighs. You then require to get down on your knees from this position and sit back onto your guy's crotch and overview his penis inside you. You can then lean in reverse to ensure that your back gets on your man's chest.

Woman roles There are a couple of various things that you can do in the Bouncing Spoon position ... You can bounce up and down on your male's crotch, although you will certainly find that this gets promptly tiring. Or you could locate it much more fun to grind on him by revolving and gyrating your hips. You can lean ahead and relax your hands on his legs or the bed to assist you to thrust onto him or grind on him.

You can attempt gradually leaning forward as well as after that jumping up as well as down if you are familiar with the Betty Rocker position.

Just make sure not to lean onward too promptly, as you will be straining your male's shaft, which can injure him! Go slow.

Male roles Your man will certainly be leaning his back up versus the head board or a wall surface, but if he is not that versatile, he can try propping himself up with cushions instead to ensure that he is not so upright. It will certainly be rather hard for him to in fact do much propelling as he will be seated.

What he can do is utilize his hands! So at least he must wrap them around you as well as massage your busts, however he can likewise use them to massage your genital areas as well as masturbate you or perhaps finger you if you are having rectal sex. He can put his hands around your waist or shoulders and also draw you down onto him with each thrust or when you are grinding if you are leaning forwards.

Tips - If you are seeking something really intimate, especially while viewing a movie/TV in bed, after that this is a terrific position, particularly when you lean right back right into your male and also he wraps his arms around you - The Bouncing Spoon sex position is great to change to from something like Reverse Cowgirl as all your guy has to do is stay up.

- As with a great deal of placements I educate, you require to lean forward/backward to discover that 'excellent place' that provides you maximum enjoyment.

10d. Lap Dance Sex Position really feel.

Performing the Lap Dance with legs together will certainly provide your male a tighter The Lap Dance sex position shares a lot alike with the Back Seat Driver position. The Lap Dance position is a sex position where your male can unwind and 'take pleasure in the program' similar to he would certainly in a strip club but he also has the choice of being a little bit more energetic.

To perform it, your man requires to muffle a comfortable couch or seat. He can sit rather far back in it and will certainly have his legs wide open. You will certainly be on your feet and also require to support right into your man. You need to order his penis as well as guide it in to your vaginal canal. As soon as he is within, you have some options:
1) You can gradually grind on your guy while he remains deep inside you.
2) You can jump up and down on him. He can help you utilizing his arms.
3) You can lean forwards or in reverse on him, depending on just how intimate you intend to make it.

Lady roles You can most likely guess from the name that the Lap Dance is mainly concerning your male's satisfaction. Keep this in mind when doing it with him.

Part of making it feel like a lap dance for your man is making it visually appealing for him. So do not be afraid to recall over your shoulder and also make eye contact with him or kiss him when you get on top.

If you lean forwards while on top of him, then you can place your hands on your knees and will certainly be extra easily able to jump on your own backwards and forwards on him. You'll discover it actually tough to jump up as well as down on him without him literally raising you up and also down if you lean in reverse. You'll discover it simpler to simply grind on him rather.

Male roles your male does not have much to do in the Lap Dance position. He can just kick back and appreciate it or he can get included by assisting to increase you backwards and forwards on him with his hands around your waistline. If you lean back into him, after that he can cover his arms around you and hold you close.

He is additionally in a wonderful position to gently massage your clitoris or finger you if you are having anal sex.

Do not forget to try the Lap Dance position with your legs open!

Tips - Some placements are all about you and also your guy pleasing you, while you don't have to do way too much job on your own. The Lap Dance is everything about him, so attempt to keep that in mind when performing it with him.

If you locate it a lot more delightful, - You can lean really far ahead to the point where you are facing the flooring.

Comments

Sex shouldn't constantly be about simply your male or just you. It's a take and give, so often your guy will certainly be doing all the work for little incentive and occasionally you will certainly be doing all the job. It's essential to keep it balanced so you both are kept pleased.

10e. Lotus Sex Position

The Lotus sex position is a truly intimate one. While it requires a little bit of versatility as well as toughness from both you, it's fairly simple.

You can see from the picture that the Lotus position creates some actually intimate, slow sex.

To enter into the Lotus sex position, your guy requires to muffle his butt with his legs went across and pulled rather enclose front of him like the standard yoga exercise position. You after that require to muffle his crotch while facing him as well as hang on to him fairly securely by covering your arms around his back and also placing your legs around his back as well to pull him in to you. Your man will additionally hang on to your rather firmly as well by placing his arms around you.

Woman roles In the Lotus position, you will certainly find it hard to do a great deal of in & out thrusting with your man. Instead, you will certainly be shaking and also grinding on your male. Yet the Lotus is not nearly making love. It's concerning getting close to your guy.

When your arms are around his back, you can massage and also scrub it. You are also in the best position to kiss your male: on the lips, cheeks, neck as well as ears.

You can additionally put your arms under his arms and reach around to grab his shoulders. This will certainly permit you to pull yourself up and down on your man while shaking as well as grinding on him.

Male roles When your male remains in the Lotus position, he will certainly discover it really tough to propelled into you. Instead he will certainly remain in an extra fluid rocking/grinding movement with you while holding you tight with his arms around your back.

One essential thing for your guy is where he places his legs. As his legs will be crossed near the ankles, it's crucial that your man does not allow you to rest or lean on them as it will certainly place a great deal of stress on them and create him some pain.

If he locates it much more comfortable, he does not need to cross his legs as well as can rather put them out directly in front of him or to the side, despite the fact that this is not practically still the Lotus.

Tips - It's an intimate position, not a 'hardcore sex position'. Utilize it for when you desire to get closer and also much more intimate with your man.

Don't fret if your male cannot cross his legs or discovers it excruciating. It's just as enjoyable when he has them straight.

You may locate that leaning backwards somewhat throughout it permits your male to give more stimulation to your G-Spot.

Remarks I discover that Lotus position can be a little unpleasant the very first couple of times you try it. As soon as you obtain made use of to it and also your guy can position his feet easily, you will certainly both truly enjoy it.

10f. Mastery Sex Position

The Mastery position is just one of those sex placements that is truly enjoyable as well as satisfying, however not that lots of people find out about it PerformingtheMasteryposition while stooping on top of your guy. To enter into the Mastery position, your guy requires to remain on the side of the bed(or on a couch), with his feet on the flooring. He needs to have both his thighs as well as butt on the bed. You then need to either kneel down onto your man's lap or squat down like in the Asian Cowgirl position. You can then cover your arms around your male's neck. Your man can try thrusting into you when you get on top of him and you can try lifting yourself backwards and forwards on him, but you'll find that it's much easier to grind and also rock on him. Girl roles In the Mastery position, you will find it simple to increase yourself backwards and forwards on him. The Mastery position is actually intimate for both of you as you are facing your male, so you can kiss him as well as keep eye contact with him. Do not forget that you can additionally put your hands around his neck and also lean right back to alter the

angle. Guy roles Your man has a choice of what he carries out in the Mastery position: 1) If he places his arms around you (when you are resting or stooping on him) then it will certainly really feel much more intimate. However when he does this, he will not be able to drive rarely at all. Rather he will certainly simply have the ability to grind up against you. 2) He can instead put his arms behind his back as well as on the bed/sofa to sustain himself and also give him take advantage of to propelled right into you.

Both options are wonderful as well as a little various. When incorporated with you either resting or stooping on him in addition to leaning right back, you have a lot of various variations of the Mastery position. Executing the Mastery position while crouching down on your male. Tips - As there are numerous different variations of the Mastery, you require to do a little experimentation to discover what you such as best.

- Maintaining eye contact with your male during the Mastery can make it extremely intimate. - Don't forget kissing your man in the Mastery position. Comments The Mastery position has a lot

of different variations as well as mixes for you to try which makes it awesome a rather versatile. You'll discover that it is fairly an intimate position as well as you can have excellent sex in it, without tiring out also quickly.

10g. See Saw Sex Position

The See Saw sex position a really fun, but quickly tiring sex position. There are no positions really comparable to it, making it quite one-of-a-kind. It additionally makes a terrific adjustment from something like Doggy Style or normal Missionary position. If you like making extreme eye call with your man during sex, performing the See Saw is great. To get involved in the See Saw position with your guy, begin by having him sit down on the bed. You after that need to sit onto his lap while encountering him. Next spread your legs out broad to ensure that you are comfortable. You currently require to lean in reverse and place your arms either on his shoulders or behind you. This position enables you to either move up and also down on his penis or grind forwards and also backwards on him all while facing your man.

Woman roles

When in the See Saw, you can pump your legs to move up and down on your guy's cock. But this will tire you out rapidly, your other option is to grind forwards as well as backwards with his penis inside you.

To grind forwards and backwards, you can utilize your hips along with using your arms put on his shoulders or wrapped around the rear of his neck. While you will certainly invest the majority of your time leaning backwards in the See Saw position, do not neglect to lean forwards and hold him close to make it much more intimate for both of you.

Male roles

When in the See Saw position, your guy won't literally have the ability to propelled right into you. He can help to raise you up and down on him by putting his arms under your upper legs as opposed to behind him, however like your legs, his arms will get tired of this quite quickly. If he is not lifting you up and down then he can use them to assist you grind on him by pressing you forwards and also backwards.

The real sexual intercourse element of the See Saw, your male can additionally quickly make eye call with you throughout it.

If he locates it to be a little bit of a strain on his back, after that your male can attempt leaning in reverse a little bit or evening placing pillows under his lower back to offer some support.

Tips

Don't seem like you need to execute the See Saw completely, doing a variant of it is completely fine (like getting on your knees rather than taking a seat into his lap).

Don't hesitate to lean right back (just ensure you don't overstrain your man's penis!). You can lean completely back till you are practically lying on your back on the bed which will make it resemble you are doing the Seat with him.

Comments

I like the See Saw. It's simple (provided your male does not have a bad back) and it's fairly different from a lot of various other positions, making it excellent for when I intend to flavor things up a little bit.

10h. Side Ride Sex Position

The Side Ride sex position is generally just a variant of the regular Asian Cowgirl position. It's extremely very easy to perform as well as is excellent if you like getting on top of your guy during sex.

To get into the Side Ride position, your male requires to rest on his back like he would during the Cowgirl position. He must flex his knees slightly so that he can place his feet on the bed to offer him some leverage for propelling right into you. You then require to muffle your man's lap, allowing him to enter you. But rather than facing him or having your back to him, you are mosting likely to be sitting sideways on him. This means that you can remain on him with your feet on either the left side or the ideal side of him.

Lady roles

When in the Side Ride position, you have a number of choices. You can stretch you legs out fairly directly so that your male is doing many of the work if you like. If you bring your feet closer in by bending your knees, you will certainly be able to press on your own up as well as down on him. Try leaning forward a little bit in the direction of your knees to make sure that you take several of your weight off your man.

To help you balance on your own, attempt putting your hands on your knees or on him. You can put them on the bed if you are leaning really far forwards.

Ensure to trying out resting on either side of your man to see what side you like.

Man roles

As I said formerly, your guy ought to have his legs slightly curved to offer him some take advantage of for thrusting up into you. This is all he needs to do actually. If he discovers it easy to do, then he can lean to either side simply a little bit to transform the angle of entry somewhat. He can slip a hand under your thighs to start rubbing your clit if you are having anal sex with your man.

Tips

- You don't need to rest perfectly to the side of your man (at a right angle to him). Attempt differing exactly how you remain on him (i.e. with your feet close his head down to having your feet by his feet.

- The Side Ride is great for those that likewise like rectal sex.

- It's additionally simple to grind on your man in the Side Ride position.

10i. Side Saddle Sex Position

When you want to take control and want your man to just relax and take it easy during sex, the Side Saddle position is great for. It's an excellent position to move to after you have actually been offering him a blowjob.

To establish it up, your man requires to rest on his back on the bed. He needs to have his butt at the edge of the bed with his legs hanging over it with his feet on the flooring. He has an option of just how he places his legs. Either together or expanded as well as open. You will certainly be dominating your man with your back to him. You can muffle top of him while spreading your legs if his legs are shut as well as together. If he has his legs open then you need to sit on top of him with your legs closed and together.

You may locate it hard to carry out the Side Saddle position if your bed is actually reduced to the floor or really high above the floor.

Woman roles

When you remain in the Side Saddle position you will certainly be using your legs to move yourself up and down on his penis. This makes the Side Saddle a great position for executing some Sexercise! You don't have to just bounce up and down on him, otherwise you'll tire yourself out. You can additionally sit right down on him and also just begin grinding on him, moving backwards and forwards. You can put your hands on your guy's legs to aid equilibrium yourself.

When you are straddling him with your legs open or with your legs closed, you may find that you prefer it either. Attempt both to see what you favor.

Guy roles

If you desire, you can make the Side Saddle all about your man and also he does not have to do anything except simply lie there. Yet if he wants after that he can returned right into you. He'll find it a whole lot easier to propel right into you when he has his legs strongly grown on the flooring.

Your guy can additionally place his hands on your midsection to assist raise you backwards and forwards on him. If you are grinding on him, while he is inside you, then he can aid to relocate you forwards as well as in reverse.

You can likewise perform the Side Saddle position with your legs open, located outdoors your males.

Tips

- You need to attempt changing your position on your man, from leaning quite far back towards him to leaning quite far forwards to ensure that you are facing in the direction of the floor.

- The Side Saddle is ideal for those that delight in anal sex.

If you want you can use your fingers to masturbate yourself or even finger yourself if you are having anal sex, -.

10j. Couch Surprise Sex Position

The Sofa Surprise sex position seems like that you can only do it when on a sofa, but you can do it on an armchair, in bed or perhaps on the floor. In several ways it's really comparable to the Asian Cowgirl.

The Sofa Surprise is a wonderful position to attempt our anywhere there is a couch or armchair!

For you and your guy to enter the Sofa Surprise position, your guy requires to sit down on a couch as he generally would. You after that need to squat below a standing position on the couch while dealing with towards him so that he can enter you. You will certainly be bowing fairly far down, so you will certainly require a little bit of adaptability or else it will be awkward. Your man will need to sit against the headboard and can put a few pillows behind himself for support if you are doing the Sofa Surprise on a bed. If you are doing it on the flooring, then he just needs to sit up versus a wall surface.

Girl roles

Your basic movement will just be up and down using your legs when you are in the Sofa Surprise position with your man. You'll find that this motion can get exhausting fairly quickly. To assist elevate on your own up and down, place your arms around the back of your male's neck.

If you feel like you require a rest, after that simply rest right down on your guy's lap while he is inside you and also grind on him by pushing your hips forwards and in reverse over him.

Guy roles

Your male can be extremely lazy and also simply sit there while you do everything. If he does then you are going to quickly tire out. To help you out, he can put his hands underneath your butt and assistance to raise you up. If he is holding on tightly), he can also help to lift you up by putting his hands on your waist (but this can be a little sore for you.

If you are resting right down on your man, grinding on him, then he can place his hands below your shoulders and also clinch you, pulling your downwards for enhanced call and also rubbing.

Tips
Do not try it if you have bad knees!

If you find it also difficult to execute the Sofa Surprise with your male, then simply attempt performing it while on your knees as opposed to getting on your feet. Getting on your knees likewise allows you to be closer to your male as well.

Comments

The Sofa Surprise position is not a position that's easy to carry out with your male. It takes a great little bit of versatility in your legs as well as a little strength also to maintain raising on your own up and down. Try it once yourself prior to determining whether you like it

Chapter 11.69 Sex Positions

Oral sex is among the most pleasurable parts of obtaining physical with your man. That's why we included these different 69 positions! The 69 sex position is wonderful for those that such as to both offer as well as obtain oral sex. Yet there is greater than one method to do the sixty 9 with your man.. Conventional 69 Position, 69 Suspended Position, Face Off Position

11a. Conventional 69 Sex Position

Because both partners are getting a ton of oral action from each other, the 69 sex position is one of the world's most It works so well. Although this is not a penetrative sex position like the Mongolian Smurf position, it's definitely one worth recognizing.

In this image, the man is on top, but if you scroll down the page, you can see one with the girl on the top.

To perform it, you need to lie on your bed on your side and face in the opposite direction to your partner that will certainly likewise be pushing his side. This means that your head will certainly be right by his penis as well as testicles, while his head will certainly be right by your vaginal area. You then require to start giving your guy a blowjob while likewise functioning his spheres with your hands/mouth. At the same time, he requires to be performing cunnilingus on you. This common pleasuring of each other can be intimate and really satisfying at the same time for both of you.

Girl roles

You just need to give your man a blowjob as you normally would when you are in the 69 position. If you are interested in making it a great blowjob, then make sure to use some of the se bj tips and oral sex techniques to spice things up a bit. Don't neglect to likewise pay attention to his balls too. If you find that your mouth is beginning to get sore or exhausted when giving him a blowjob, feel free to switch to providing him a handjob rather.

Man roles

When he's in the 69 position, your guy's job is to perform cunnilingus on you. You might need to give him some pointers if he's not very good at it. You might discover it unpleasant to approach it like you are his instructor. You'll discover it simpler to just be more singing when he is striking a great area, attempt saying things like, "Right there!" or "That feels impressive!" when he is licking you in a really pleasurable means.

Your male can also utilize his fingers when your are 69ing with him.

The 69 is an excellent way to finish sexual activity before you begin making love.

Tips

The 69 is ideal for throughout foreplay with your male.

You don't have to only push your side throughout the 69. You can lie on your back while your man is supporting himself above you on his hands and knees if you like. Or he can rest on his back, while you are above him.

When drawing your man's penis, you can attempt getting the base of it with one hand to prevent it from going too far right into your throat.

It you desire more intense stimulation from your guy, get him to wrap his arms around your midsection to pull you in on top of him.

If you do not like the suggestion of kissing your guy right after carrying out the 69 on him, then ensure to maintain some mints/gum close by to cover any type of preferences you don't want.

If you feel that you are about to orgasm, then take your man's penis out of your mouth. Individuals usually clench their jaws as they orgasm. When his cock is in your mouth, this is why you do not want to orgasm!

If your male is typically rather quick to have an orgasm, after that it may be an excellent suggestion to allow him consume you out for a while initially, before you start offering him a blowjob. By doing this you both obtain a ton of pleasure out of it as well as your are not left desiring.

Comments

The huge majority of people (both males and females) appreciate carrying out the 69 position The Race To 69 '. It's primarily just a simple sex video game where you attempt to make your male climax prior to he makes you climax. The champion is the individual who orgasms last. It's a little ridiculous however it's wonderful for spicing points up as well as keeping sex fun.

11b. 69 Suspended Sex Position

The put on hold 69 sex position is a very exotic one. It's not meant for most couples as it's just so challenging and exhausting to perform. But if you can pull it off with your male, then you are going to have a great deal of enjoyable. Prior to you even try the put on hold, 69 you require to see to it that both you as well as your male are strong enough to do it.

Your guy is mosting likely to be lugging all your weight, while you are upside-down. In general, you man demands to be fairly muscular to do it, while you require to be quite tiny, or else you will certainly place a huge pressure on his back and also neck.

To start off, I advise that your man lies down on his back on the bed, with his feet over the side of the bed to make sure that they are touching the flooring. You then need to get involved in the regular 69 position in addition to him. When you remain in the 69 position, make certain that your legs are rather close together to make sure that they are practically pressing your guy's head

The very first test (prior to he attempts to stand) is to see if you are both able to perform it while your male is simply resting upright on the bed. So your guy needs to stay up. He will certainly require to use one hand to push himself upwards, while utilizing his various other to steady himself. You need to keep your legs wrapped around the back of his neck and arms wrapped around his waist to keep yourself in position and to prevent yourself from sliding down.

Girl roles

When you are in the suspended 69 you will certainly be doing fairly a lot of work simply to keep on your own ready. For the majority of girls, that's the main point that they focus on.

I constantly advise that you begin the put on hold 69 from a seated position and also try it out there first momentarily or 2 to see if it's comfortable before your guy stays up. When you are inverted, it's going to take a little while for you to get seasoned. As opposed to taking your male's penis right into your mouth to give him a blowjob, you must try licking it and kissing it and also only take the tip of it into your mouth. This is due to the fact that you won't have your arms cost-free to help you control exactly how deep you take it.

Once you fit trying the suspended 69 from a seated position, it's time to try it with your male standing.

Man roles

Your male needs to first and foremost focus on keeping you suspended and seeing to it that he remains stable, to ensure that neither of you injure yourselves. Like I already stated, he needs to try the suspended 69 with you first from a seated position and afterwards later on from a standing position. Your man requires to be mindful to ensure that you don't slide too far downwards. He can do this by getting to down as well as holding you by your shoulders.

When in the suspended 69, he simply needs to slowly lick you out using his tongue. Broad, soft strokes are best for this. He doesn't require to perform any kind of 'crazy' moves on you as he requires to concentrate much more on making sure he has a company hold.

Tips

It's really tiring, indicating that you can generally just do it momentarily or 2 with your male.

Both partners require to know what they are doing in advance to prevent any type of problems. They likewise need to be fairly in shape.

Try to use your hands around his midsection to take the majority of your weight, or else you will certainly be placing a substantial strain on the back of his neck with your legs.

You might discover that doing simultaneous oral sex on each other is quite difficult. You might locate it simpler if you take it in turns. 1 minute of offering your man a blowjob, after that 1 minute of him consuming you out or something similar.

Remarks

I directly see the put on hold 69 as even more of a novelty sex position, than one for you to obtain a lot of enjoyment out of. If you find that sex is getting boring for you and your man, the suspended 69 is a killer way to make it more exciting again. While a great deal of couples don't actually obtain a lots of enjoyment out of it, it's so different, unique and 'around' that it's just really refreshing.

11c. Face Off Sex Position

The Face Off sex position is 69 position that the majority of guys will certainly have never experienced ... making it excellent for surprising your guy when you really feel that sex is starting to get a little boring.

To enter into position for the Face Off, your guy requires to sit down on either the floor or on the bed with his legs out directly with his body upright. You after that require to stand in front of him, dealing with parallel to make sure that your butt is in his face. Maintain your feet outside his. Next your demand to bend right over to begin offering your guy a blowjob. You will be exposing yourself so that it's really easy for your man to perform cunnilingus on you and eat you out.

The Face Off is an actually enjoyable variation of the normal 69 position.

Girl roles
When in the Face Off position, you simply need to focus on 3 things:
1) Staying Comfortable
2) Keeping Your Balance
3) Giving Him A Wonderful Blowjob
1) Staying comfortable is actually rather easy. If you keep your legs straight, then they will certainly get sore rather quick. If you bend your knees, you'll find that you can stay in the Face Off position for much longer. Furthermore, if you need to pause, then do not hesitate to stand up straight, while your guy keeps pleasuring you. For some, it takes some time to get used to having your head upside down.
2) Keeping your balance is additionally relatively very easy. Just put your hands on the flooring and spread your legs quite broad.

Man roles
Your male has a much easier work in the Face Off position. He has 2 things he requires to concentrate on:
1) Helping You to Stay Balanced
2) Giving You Great Cunnilingus
1) To aid you maintain balanced, your male just requires to delicately place his hands around your legs or back and also hold you in position.

2) Some guys don't pay sufficient attention to pleasing their woman, while others do. If your man is not doing an excellent task, then there is a method to offer him some assistance. Simply begin informing him what you like as he is doing it. Say things like, "That really feels outstanding" or "Right there" or "Don't stop". This positive reinforcement will allow him recognize to keep doing the important things you such as.

Tips
If you find it hard bending over, then position your feet behind your man's back so that you do not need to flex over as a lot.

You can likewise use the Face off position specifically for getting foreplay from your man. This indicates you do not need to lean over so much or you can also stand completely upright throughout it.

Performing the Face Off in the reverse direction (by having your male stand and also lean over while you sit down) does not work so well. It makes it very hard for him to do cunnilingus on you.

11d. Golden Gate Sex Position

The Golden Gate sex position is a 69 position so that both you and your male can perform oral sex on each other at the same time. It's an extremely tough to execute position
To execute the Golden Gate position, your male needs to lie down on the bed on his back. He then requires to flexes his knees and also put his feet on the bed to keep himself balanced. You after that need to jump on your knees, straight over your man's mouth to make sure that you have your back to his body. He can start licking you out as well as carrying out cunnilingus on you. You currently need to lean backwards, just like you would in the Acrobat position.

Executing the Golden Gate is tough, unless you are incredibly flexible.
As you lean backwards, maintain your knees on the bed and curve your back to bring your head down towards his crotch to start giving him a blowjob. Prolong you arms and also place your hands on the bed to keep on your own well balanced.
If this all sounds very tough, then you're right, it is. That's why I consider it a lot more an uniqueness position than a major sex position.

Girl roles
All you require to do in the Golden Gate position is simply remain in this unpleasant, curved position and also offer your man a blowjob while he carries out cunnilingus on you. It can be fairly hard, yet you also need to prevent yourself from taking your man too deeply to quit him from accidentally choking you.

Man roles
Your man has really little to do in the Golden Gate position other than simply eating you out. He may feel like propelling into your mouth in this position, however he should not. He must simply remain still as well as let you do all the embedding instance he chokes/hurts you by mistake.
To aid maintain you balanced, your male can wrap his arms around your legs.
Aside from that though, he won't be doing a great deal.

Tips
It's truly hard to carry out. Simply getting involved in position can be a great deal of work for some.
You feel like you have extremely little control and that one wrong relocation can have your guy's penis really far down your throat.

If you wish to attempt every action as well as position in guide, put the Golden Gate as one of your last. The majority of pairs locate that it's unworthy the initiative, despite the fact that it does look truly exotic.

Comments

I don't such as the Golden Gate sex position. Its way too much work as well as for me sex is meant to be very easy as well as fun.